BMW
SERVICE • REPAIR HANDBOOK
1600 AND 2002 SERIES • 1966-1976

By

JIM COMBS

JEFF ROBINSON
Editor and Publisher

Published by

CLYMER PUBLICATIONS

*World's largest publisher of books devoted exclusively to
automobiles and motorcycles.*

222 NORTH VIRGIL AVENUE, LOS ANGELES, CALIFORNIA 90004

FIRST EDITION
First Printing June, 1973
Second Printing September, 1973

SECOND EDITION
Revised to include 1974-1976 models
First Printing September, 1976
Second Printing July, 1977

Printed in U. S. A.

ISBN: 0-89287-113-X

CONTENTS

CHAPTER ONE

GENERAL INFORMATION

This manual provides maintenance information on the Bavarian Motor Works (BMW) 1600 and 2002 Series of cars imported into the United States from 1966 through 1976. The 1600 models include the 1600 and the 1600-2. The 2002 models include the 2002, 2002A, 2002ti, and 2002tii. Except for differences in bore, stroke, piston shape, emission control devices, and carburetion, the engine design is essentially the same between models and has not significantly changed over the years.

All models have a 4-cylinder, inline engine with a single overhead camshaft. The engine is mounted at an angle for styling purposes. Carburetion includes single downdraft, 2-stage downdraft, twin sidedraft, and fuel injection, depending on the model and year. Transmissions used are a 4-speed manual and a 3-speed automatic. Details on the different engines, carburetors, and transmissions are covered in this manual along with details of all other major systems.

MANUAL ORGANIZATION

In this manual most dimensions and capacities are expressed in inch units familiar to U.S. mechanics, as well as in metric units. Where conversion to inches could introduce errors in critical dimensions, only metric measure is specified, and vice versa. In any case, *metric tools are required to work on the BMW*.

This chapter provides general information for the BMW 1600 and 2002 Series. Figure 1 shows the location of all identification tags and **Table 1** provides general dimensions and weights.

Table 1   **GENERAL DIMENSIONS & WEIGHTS**

Overall length	166.5 in. (4.23m) ①
Overall width	62.5 in. (1.59m)
Height (unladen)	55.5 in. (1.41m)
Wheelbase	98.375 in. (2.50m)
Track	
Front	52.75 in. (1.348m)
Rear	52.75 in. (1.348m)
Turning circle diameter	34 ft. 2 in. (10.4m)
Ground clearance (laden)	6.3125 in. (160mm)
Curb weight (empty)	
1600	2,050 lb. (932 kg)
2002 (early)	2,073 lb. (942 kg)
(includes 2002A & 2002ti)	
2002 (later)	2,183 lb. (990 kg)
2002tii	2,226 lb. (1,010 kg)
Maximum load	880 lb. (400 kg)
① 176.0 in. for 1975-1976 models.	

Chapter Two covers all periodic lubrication and routine maintenance required to keep your car in top running condition.

Chapter Three provides methods and suggestions for finding and fixing troubles fast. Troubleshooting procedures discuss typical symptoms and logical methods to pinpoint the trouble. It also discusses test equipment useful for both preventive maintenance and troubleshooting.

Chapter Four provides instructions for tuning the engine along with necessary specifications.

Subsequent chapters describe specific systems such as the engine, transmission, and electrical system. Each provides complete disassembly, repair and assembly procedures in easy to follow step-by-step form.

SERVICE HINTS

The procedures used in this manual avoid the use of special tools and test equipment wherever possible. When necessary, special tools and test equipment are illustrated, either in actual use or alone. Special tools may be ordered and purchased through BMW dealers. However, a well-equipped mechanic may find he can substitute similar tools or make his own to fulfill a requirement.

Recommendations are occasionally made to refer service or maintenance to a BMW dealer or a specialist in a particular field. In these cases, work will probably be done more quickly and economically than if the owner performs it himself.

When ordering parts from a dealer or other parts distributor, always order by engine and chassis number. Write the numbers down and carry them in your wallet. Also, record the numbers stamped on your keys to permit replacement in case of loss.

Throughout this manual, keep the following conventions in mind: "front" refers to the front of the car; "left" and "right" refer to a person sitting in the car facing forward. The cylinders are numbered from 1 to 4 starting at the front of the engine. The abbreviation TDC means top dead center (on the compression stroke) of a piston within a cylinder. BTDC means before top dead center; ATDC means after top dead center.

MODEL IDENTIFICATION

Manufacturer's Identification Plate

See **Figure 1**. The manufacturer's plate is in the engine compartment on the rear right-hand side.

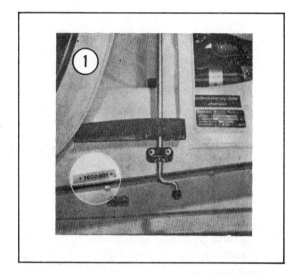

Chassis Number

See Figure 1. The chassis number is in the engine compartment on the right side of the firewall next to the lock.

Engine Number

See **Figure 2**. The engine number is on the rear left-hand side of the crankcase above the starter.

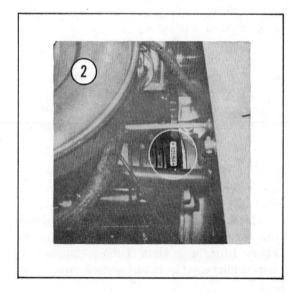

CHAPTER TWO

MAINTENANCE AND LUBRICATION

A regular program of lubrication and preventive maintenance is necessary to ensure good performance and dependability. This chapter suggests a maintenance program for a car driven by an average driver. One driven harder than average may require more frequent attention. On the other hand, rust, dirt, and corrosion may cause unnecessary damage to a seldom-used vehicle. BMW recommends that their cars be serviced (oil and filter change, plus safety checks) a minimum of twice a year or at the intervals stated in **Table 1**, whichever comes first. Whether performed by the owner or by a BMW dealer, regular routine attention helps avoid expensive repairs.

The schedule recommended in this chapter includes routine checks which are easily performed at each fuel stop; periodic checks to be performed at each oil change, and periodic maintenance to prevent future troubles. Table 1 summarizes all periodic maintenance required.

ROUTINE CHECKS

The following checks should be performed at each fuel stop.

1. Check engine oil. Oil should be checked with the engine warm and on level ground. See **Figure 1** for the location of the oil dipstick (1) and oil filler cap (2) on carburetted models, and

Figure 2 for the location of these items on the fuel injected Model 2002tii. Add oil if required.

CAUTION
Do not operate the vehicle when the oil level is below the lower mark on the dipstick. Also, do not add oil of another make unless a complete oil change, including filter, is made. Damage to the engine could result.

NOTE: *Slightly more than 3 pints of oil are required to bring the oil level from the lower mark to the upper mark on the dipstick. Do not overfill.*

2. Check battery electrolyte level. It should be level with the bar which can be seen in each cell

Table 1   LUBRICATION AND MAINTENANCE SUMMARY

Interval	Item	Check/ Replenish	Check/ Service	Lubricate	Replace
Fuel stop	Engine oil	X			
	Battery electrolyte	X			
	Brake/clutch fluid	X			
	Tire pressure	X			
	Engine coolant	X			
	Windshield washer	X			
	Leak check		X		
4,000 or 6,000 ① miles	Engine oil				X
	Oil filter				X
	Air filter		X		
8,000 or 12,500 ① miles	Transmission oil	X			
	Steering gear oil	X			
	Differential/rear axles	X			
	Hinges/pivots/locks			X	
	Distributor			X	
	Wheel rotation and balance		X		
	Air filter				X
	Evaporation control system		X		
	Fuel pump filter		X		
	Spark plugs				X
	Ignition contact points				X
	Engine timing		X		
	Valve clearance adjustment		X		
	Belts and hoses		X		
	Pre-heat valve		X		
	Brakes		X		
	Carburetor adjustment		X		
	Safety check		X		
	Exhaust manifold nuts		X		
	Rear half axles and universal joints		X		
	Wheel bearings		X		
	Exhaust gas recirculation system (EGR system)		X		
20,000 miles	Transmission oil				X

(continued)

① 1975-1976 models.

2

3. Using a screwdriver or other suitable tool as a lever, turn the induction unit counterclockwise to disengage the bayonet-type catch. Remove the unit.

4. Clean the filter unit at the bottom of the induction unit, then replace unit, tighten catch securely, and replace and clamp fuel line.

Main Fuel Filter

Replace the main fuel filter at the intervals shown in Table 1. Be sure to follow the flow instructions given on the filter element. See **Figure 22**.

Torques

At the intervals stated in Table 1, tighten the following nuts and bolts to the specified torques:

    a. Engine mounts, right and left (18 ft.-lb.)

    b. Intake manifold (18 ft.-lb.)

    c. Carburetor-to-intake manifold (10 ft.-lb.)

    d. Fuel pump (9 ft.-lb.)

    e. Exhaust mountings (24 ft.-lb.)

Clutch Drive Plate

The clutch does not require maintenance and is self-adjusting. However, at the intervals given in Table 1, wear of the clutch drive plate should be measured to determine if replacement is required. See **Figure 23**. Push the operating lever toward the front of the car until it contacts the stop on the clutch slave cylinder and measure distance (A). When new, thrust rod travel (A) is 0.67-0.75 in. (17-19mm). As the clutch plate wears, the distance becomes smaller. The minimum allowable distance is 0.2 in. (5mm). When the minimum travel is reached, the clutch drive plate must be replaced.

Headlight Beam Adjustment

At the intervals given in Table 1, or earlier if headlights appear to be improperly adjusted, have the headlights checked and adjusted, if required, by your BMW dealer or a headlight specialist.

LUBRICANTS

Use of the proper lubricants is a very important part of automotive maintenance. Incorrect lubricants can lead to improper operation and accelerated wear. See **Table 3** for the lubricants recommended for use in BMW automobiles. See **Table 4** for capacities. **Figure 24** is a typical lubrication chart.

OIL FILTER

Two types of filters have been used. One type has a replaceable element within a permanent

Table 3   RECOMMENDED LUBRICANTS

Use	Recommendation
Engine oil	High quality heavy duty (HD) motor oil
Manual transmission	SAE 80 transmission oil (NOT hypoid gear oil)
Automatic transmission	"DEXRON" type automatic transmission fluid
Steering gear	SAE 90 hypoid gear oil
Differential	SAE 90 hypoid gear oil
Wheel bearings	Bearing grease with a melting point above 500°F
Hinges, pivot points, latches	Graphite-based oil
Brake fluid reservoir	ATE "S" blue brake fluid, or Castrol Disc or Girling green brake fluid

Table 4   FLUID CAPACITIES

Item	Capacity
Fuel tank	13.5 U.S. gallons
Cooling system, including heater	1.5 U.S. gallons
Engine oil	5 U.S. quarts (including 0.5 quart in filter)
Manual transmission	2.1 U.S. pints (3 pints in 5-speed transmission)
Automatic transmission	Approximately 3.5 U.S. pints (9.5 pints for new transmission at first filling)
Differential	1.9 U.S. pints
Steering gear box	0.64 U.S. pints

body, as shown in **Figure 25**. The other is a screw on, throw-away unit as shown in **Figure 26**. Both filters are full-flow with the pressure relief valve either built into the filter body or filter housing. Change the oil filter whenever the engine oil is changed.

Replacement (Replaceable Element)

1. See Figure 25. Unscrew and remove the bolt (13). Remove the sealing ring (5) and the filter case (7) from upper part of body.

2. Discard filter element. Clean all parts with suitable solvent.

3. Inspect condition of case and sealing ring at top of case and ring at bottom of bolt. Repair is by replacement.

4. Install new element into case. Install sealing ring, bolt and ring. Tighten bolt securely. Do not overtighten as leakage may result.

5. Add oil to the proper level. Start engine and inspect oil filter at the top seal and bottom bolt for signs of leaks.

Replacement (Screw-on Unit)

1. See Figure 26. Use a filter wrench to unscrew and remove the filter. Discard the filter.

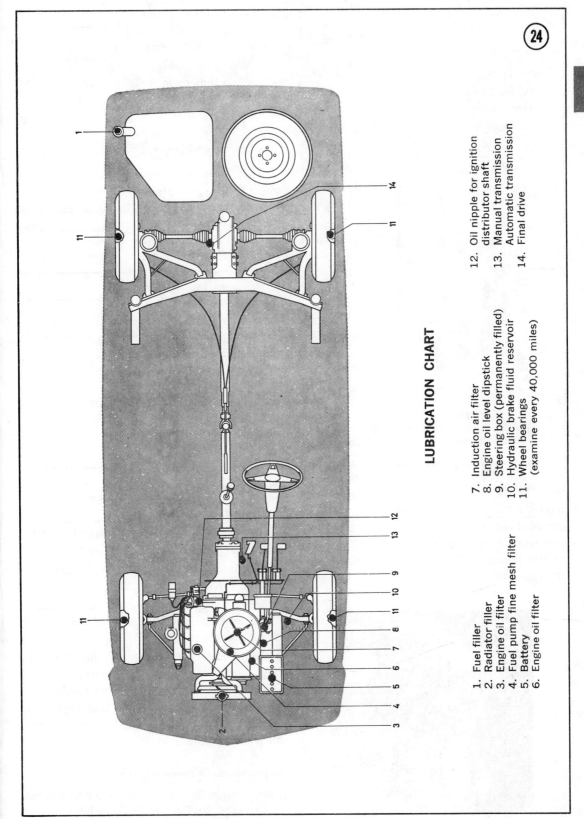

LUBRICATION CHART

1. Fuel filler
2. Radiator filler
3. Engine oil filter
4. Fuel pump fine mesh filter
5. Battery
6. Engine oil filter

7. Induction air filter
8. Engine oil level dipstick
9. Steering box (permanently filled)
10. Hydraulic brake fluid reservoir
11. Wheel bearings
    (examine every 40,000 miles)

12. Oil nipple for ignition
    distributor shaft
13. Manual transmission
    Automatic transmission
14. Final drive

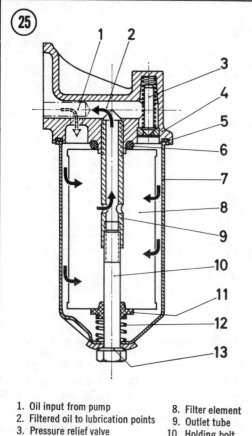

1. Oil input from pump
2. Filtered oil to lubrication points
3. Pressure relief valve
4. Upper part of body
5. Sealing ring
6. Rubber sealing ring
7. Filter casing
8. Filter element
9. Outlet tube
10. Holding bolt
11. Rubber seal
12. Spring
13. Sealing ring

2. Apply a trace of oil to the new sealing ring. Install the sealing ring and the filter to the housing by threading the filter on. Do not overtighten as leakage may result.

3. Fill the engine to the proper level with oil, start engine, and inspect oil filter for leaks at the top of the filter.

OIL PRESSURE SENDING UNIT

The oil pressure sending unit is connected electrically to the warning indicator on the dashboard instrument panel. The lamp lights when the oil pressure falls to a critical level. Normal oil pressure is about 59 psi at 4,000 rpm.

If the lamp lights during normal operation, stop the engine immediately and determine the cause of the low oil pressure indication. Check the level of the engine oil first and replenish as required. If the engine oil condition and level are normal, check the connection to the sending unit and the lamp. If normal, replace sending unit with a new one. If this does not solve the problem, remove the sump plug and drain engine oil. Install new oil filter or element, as described above, and fill the sump with new oil. If abnormal condition persists, the problem is probably in the oil pump or there is a blockage in the oil lines. If this is the case, service the oil pump and clean out oil passages, which requires engine removal and disassembly. Refer to Chapter Five for procedures.

CHAPTER THREE

TROUBLESHOOTING

Troubleshooting the BMW can be relatively simple if done logically. The first step is to define the trouble symptoms as closely as possible. Subsequent steps involve testing and analyzing areas which could cause the symptoms.

Procedures in this chapter cover typical symptoms and describe logical methods of isolation. These are not the only methods. There may be several approaches to solving a problem, but all methods must have one thing in common—a logical, systematic approach.

TROUBLESHOOTING EQUIPMENT

The following equipment is necessary to properly troubleshoot the engine and it's components.

1. Voltmeter, ammeter, and ohmmeter
2. Hydrometer
3. Compression tester
4. Vacuum gauge
5. Tachometer
6. Dwell meter
7. Timing light
8. Exhaust gas analyzer

Items 1 through 7 are essential. Item 8 is necessary for exhaust emission control compliance. The following is a brief description of the function of each instrument.

Voltmeter, Ammeter, and Ohmmeter

For testing the ignition and electrical systems, a good voltmeter is required. The range of the meter should cover from 0 to 20 volts, and have an accuracy of $\pm$ ½ volt.

The ohmmeter measures electrical resistance and is required to check continuity (open- and short-circuits), and to test fuses and lights.

The ammeter measures electrical current. One for automotive use should cover 0 - 10 amperes and 0 - 100 amperes. An ammeter is useful for checking battery charging and starting current. The starter and generator inspection and repair procedures use an ammeter to check for shorted windings.

Hydrometer

A hydrometer gives an indication of battery condition and charge by measuring the specific gravity of the electrolyte in each cell.

Compression Tester

The compression tester measures pressure buildup in each cylinder. The results, when properly interpreted, can indicate general cylinder and valve condition. To perform the compression check, proceed as follows:

1. Run the engine until normal operating temperature is reached, then shut it off.

2. Block the choke and throttle in the wide open position.

3. Remove all spark plugs.

4. Connect compression tester to one cylinder, following manufacturer's instructions.

5. Have an assistant crank the engine for at least 4 turns.

6. Remove the tester and record the reading.

7. Repeat the above steps for each cylinder.

If the compression readings register 135 to 150 psi and do not differ from each other by more than 10 psi, the rings and valves are in good condition. If all cylinders are uniformly low or high, the compression tester may be inaccurate. The important point is the difference between the readings.

Compression Defects

Low Compression in One Cylinder. If a low reading (10% or more) is obtained on one cylinder, it indicates valve or ring trouble. To determine which, pour about a teaspoon of engine oil through the spark plug hole onto the top of the piston. Turn the engine over once to clear some of the excess oil, then take another compression test and record the reading. If the compression returns to normal, the valves are good but the rings are defective on that cylinder. If compression does not increase, the valves require servicing.

Low Compression in Two Adjacent Cylinders. This may indicate that the head gasket has blown between the cylinders and that gases are leaking from one cylinder to the other. Replace the head gasket as described in Chapter Six.

To isolate the trouble more closely, compare the compression readings with vacuum gauge readings as described below.

Vacuum Gauge

The vacuum gauge is easy to use, but difficult for an inexperienced mechanic to interpret. The results, when considered with other findings, can provide valuable clues to possible trouble.

Connect the vacuum gauge with a T-connector in the hose from the carburetor to the vacuum advance on the distributor. Vacuum reading should be steady at 18-22 in. at idle

speed. Subtract 1 in. from reading for every 1,000 feet of elevation above sea level. **Figure 1** shows numerous typical readings with interpretations. Results are not conclusive without comparing to other test results, such as compression readings.

Fuel Pressure Gauge

This instrument is vital for evaluating fuel pump performance. Often a vacuum gauge and fuel pressure gauge are combined into one instrument.

Tachometer

A tachometer is essential for tuning engines with exhaust emission control systems. Ignition timing and carburetor adjustments must be performed at specified idle speed. The best instrument for this purpose is one with a range of 0 - 1,000 or 0 - 2,000 rpm. Extended range (0 - 6,000) instruments lack accuracy at lower speeds. The instrument should be capable of detecting changes of 25 rpm.

Dwell Meter

A dwell meter measures the distance in degrees of cam rotation that the distributor breaker points remain closed while the engine is running. Since this angle is determined by breaker point gap, dwell angle is an accurate indication of point gap. Many tachometers incorporate a dwell meter as well. Follow the instrument manufacturer's instructions to measure dwell.

Stroboscopic Timing Light

This instrument permits accurate engine timing. By flashing a light at the precise instant that cylinder No. 1 fires, the position of the crankshaft pulley at that instant can be seen. Marks on the pulley are lined up with the crankcase pointer to time the engine.

Suitable lights are neon bulb and xenon strobe types. Neon bulb timing lights are difficult to see and must be used in dimly lit areas. Xenon strobe timing lights can be used in bright sunlight. Use the light according to the manufacturer's instructions.

In some models, the timing mark is located on the flywheel rather than on the crankshaft

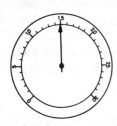

1. NORMAL READING
Reads 15 in. at idle.

2. LATE IGNITION TIMING
About 2 inches too low at idle.

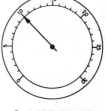

3. LATE VALVE TIMING
About 4 to 8 inches low at idle.

3

4. INTAKE LEAK
Low steady reading.

5. NORMAL READING
Drops to 2, then rises to 25 when accelerator is rapidly depressed and released.

6. WORN RINGS, DILUTED OIL
Drops to 0, then rises to 18 when accelerator is rapidly depressed and released.

7. STICKING VALVE(S)
Normally steady. Intermittently flicks downward about 4 in.

8. LEAKY VALVE
Regular drop about 2 inches.

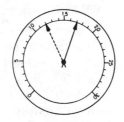

9. BURNED OR WARPED VALVE
Regular, evenly spaced down-scale flick about 4 in.

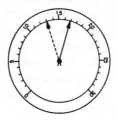

10. WORN VALVE GUIDES
Oscillates about 4 in.

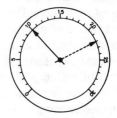

11. WEAK VALVE SPRINGS
Violent oscillation (about 10 in.) as rpm increases. Often steady at idle.

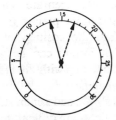

12. IMPROPER IDLE MIXTURE
Floats slowly between 13-17 in.

13. SMALL SPARK GAP or DEFECTIVE POINTS
Slight float between 14-16 in.

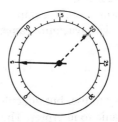

14. HEAD GASKET LEAK
Gauge floats between 5-19 in.

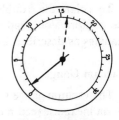

15. RESTRICTED EXHAUST SYSTEM
Normal when first started. Drops to 0 as rpm increases. May eventually rise to about 16.

pulley. For these, there is an access opening to the flywheel so that the timing mark can be seen. The timing mark on the flywheel is referenced to a point in the access opening for timing purposes, as described in Chapter Four.

Exhaust Analyzer

Of all instruments, this is the least likely to be owned by an amature mechanic. The most common type samples exhaust gases from the tailpipe and measures thermal conductivity. Since different gases conduct heat at varying rates, thermal conductivity is a good indication of gases present.

STARTER TROUBLESHOOTING

Starter system troubles are relatively easy to isolate. The following are common symptoms.

Engine Cranks Very Slowly or Not At All

Turn on the headlights. If the lights are very dim, the battery or connecting wires most likely are at fault. Check the battery with hydrometer. Check wiring for breaks, shorts, and dirty connections. If the battery and wires are all right, turn the headlights on and crank the engine. If the lights dim drastically, the starter is probably shorted to ground.

If the lights remain bright or dim slightly when cranking, the trouble may be in the starter, solenoid, or wiring. To isolate the trouble, short the two large solenoid terminals together (not to ground); if the starter cranks normally, check the solenoid and wiring to the ignition switch. If the starter still fails to crank properly, remove and test it.

Starter Turns, but Does Not Engage with Engine

Usually caused by defective pinion gear or soelnoid shifting fork. The teeth on the pinion, flywheel ring gear, or both may be worn too far to engage properly.

Starter Engages, but Will Not Disengage When Ignition Switch Is Released

Usually caused by sticking solenoid, but occasionally the pinion may jam on the flywheel. The pinion can be temporarily freed by rocking the car in fourth or fifth gear.

Loud Grinding Noises When Starter Runs

The teeth on the pinion and/or flywheel are not meshing properly or the overrunning clutch mechanism is broken. Remove the starter and examine the gear teeth and pinion drive assembly.

CHARGING SYSTEM TROUBLESHOOTING

Charging system troubles may be in the generator (alternator), voltage regulator, or fan belt. The following symptoms are typical.

Dashboard Indicator Shows Continuous Discharge

This usually means that battery charging is not taking place. Check fan belt tension. Check battery condition with hydrometer and electrical connections in the charging system. Finally, check the generator and/or voltage regulator.

Dashboard Indicator Shows Intermittent Discharge

Check fan belt tension and electrical connections. Trouble may be traced to worn generator brushes or bad commutator.

Battery Requires Frequent Addition of Water or Lamps Require Frequent Replacement

Generator (alternator) may be overcharging the battery or the voltage regulator is faulty.

Excessive Noise From the Generator (Alternator)

Check for loose mountings and/or worn bearings.

ENGINE TROUBLESHOOTING

These procedures assume the starter cranks the engine over normally. If not, refer to the *Starter* section of this chapter.

Engine Won't Start

Could be caused by the ignition or fuel system. First, determine if high voltage to spark plugs occurs. To do this, disconnect one of the spark plug wires. Hold the exposed wire terminal about ¼ to ½ in. from ground (any metal in the engine compartment) with an insulated screwdriver. Crank the engine. If sparks don't jump to ground or the sparks are very weak, the trouble may be in the ignition system. If sparks occur properly, the trouble may be in the fuel system.

Engine Misses Steadily

Use a heavily insulated tool and remove one spark plug wire at a time and ground the wire. If engine miss increases, that cylinder is working properly. Reconnect the wire and check the other spark plugs. When a wire is disconnected and engine miss remains the same, that cylinder is not firing. Check spark as described above. If no spark occurs for one cylinder only, check distributor cap, wire, and spark plug. If spark occurs properly, check compression and intake manifold vacuum.

Engine Misses Erratically at All Speeds

Intermittent trouble can be difficult to find. It could be in the ignition system, exhaust system, or fuel system. Follow troubleshooting procedures for these systems to isolate the trouble.

Engine Misses at Idle Only

Trouble could be in ignition or carburetor idle adjustment. Check idle mixture adjustment and check for restrictions in the idle circuit.

Engine Misses at High Speed Only

Trouble is in the fuel or ignition system. Check accelerator pump operation, fuel pump delivery, fuel lines, etc. Check spark plugs and wires.

Low Performance at All Speeds, Poor Acceleration

Trouble usually exists in ignition or fuel system.

Excessive Fuel Consumption

Could be caused by a number of seemingly unrelated factors. Check for clutch slippage, brake drag, defective wheel bearings, poor front end alignment, faulty ignition, leaky gas tank or lines, and carburetor condition.

Low Oil Pressure Indicated by Oil Pressure Gauge

If the oil pressure gauge shows low oil pressure with the engine running, stop the engine immediately. Coast to a stop with the clutch disengaged. The trouble may be caused by low oil level, blockage in an oil line, defective oil pump, overheated engine, or defective pressure sending switch. Check the oil level and fan belt tension. Check for a shorted oil pressure sender with an ohmmeter. Remove and clean the oil pressure relief valve. Do not re-start the engine until you know why the low indication was given and are sure the problem has been corrected.

Engine Overheats

Usually caused by trouble in the cooling system. Check the level of coolant in the radiator, condition of the fan belt, and water hoses for leaks and loose connections. Can also be caused by late ignition or valve timing.

Engine Stalls as it Warms Up

The choke valve may be stuck closed, the manifold heat control valve may be stuck, the engine idle speed may be set too low, or the emission control valve may be faulty.

Engine Stalls After Idling or Slow-Speed Driving

Can be caused by defective fuel pump, overheated engine, high carburetor float level, incorrect idle adjustment, or defective emission control valve.

Engine Stalls After High-Speed Driving

Vapor lock within the fuel lines caused by an overheated engine is the usual cause of this trouble. Inspect and service the cooling system. If the trouble persists, changing to a different fuel or shielding the fuel line from engine heat may be helpful.

Engine Backfires

Several causes can be suspect: ignition timing, overheating, excessive carbon build-up, worn ignition points, wrong heat range spark plugs, hot or sticking valves, and/or defective distributor cap.

Smoky Exhaust

Blue smoke indicates excessive oil consumption usually caused by worn rings. Black smoke indicates an excessive rich fuel mixture in the carburetor.

Excessive Oil Consumption

Can be caused by external leaks through broken seals or gaskets, or by burning oil in the combustion chambers. Check the oil pan and the front and rear of the engine for oil leaks. If the oil is not leaking externally, valve stem clearances may be excessive, piston rings may be worn, cylinder walls may be scored, rod bearings may be worn, or the vacuum-pump diaphragm may be ruptured.

Engine is Noisy

Regular Clicking Sound—Valves out of adjustment.

Ping or Chatter On Load or Acceleration—Spark knock due to low octane fuel, carbon build-up, overly advanced ignition timing, and causes mentioned under engine backfire.

Light Knock or Pound With Engine Not Under Load—Indicates worn connecting rod bearings, misaligned crank pin, and/or lack of engine oil.

Light Metallic Double Knock, Usually Heard During Idle—Worn or loose piston pin or bushing and/or lack of oil.

Chattering or Rattling During Acceleration—Worn rings, cylinder walls, low ring tension, and/or broken rings.

Hollow, Bell-like Muffled Sound When Engine is Cold—Piston slap due to worn pistons, cylinder walls, collapsed piston skirts, excessive clearances, misaligned connecting rods, and/or lack of oil.

Dull, Heavy Metallic Knock Under Load or Acceleration, Especially When Cold—Regular noise: worn main bearings; irregular noise: worn thrust bearings.

IGNITION SYSTEM TROUBLESHOOTING

The following procedures assume the battery is in good enough condition to crank the engine normally.

No Spark to One Plug

The only causes are defective distributor cap, rotor, or spark plug wire. Examine the distributor cap for moisture, dirt, carbon tracking caused by flashover, and cracks. Check condition of rotor and spark plug wire for breaks and loose connectors.

No Spark to Any Plug

This could indicate trouble in the primary or secondary ignition circuits. First remove the coil wire from the center post of the distributor. Hold the wire end about ¼ in. from ground with an insulated screwdriver. Crank the engine. If sparks are produced, the trouble is in the rotor or distributor cap. Remove the cap and check for burns, moisture, dirt, carbon tracking, cracks, etc. Check rotor for excessive burning, pitting and cracks.

If the coil does not produce any spark, check the secondary wire for a break. If the wire is good, turn the engine over so the breaker points are open. Check the points for excessive gap, burning, pitting, and loose connections. With the points open, check voltage from the coil to ground with a voltmeter or test lamp. If voltage is present, the coil is probably defective. Have it checked or substitute a coil known to be good.

If voltage is not present, check wire connections to coil and distributor. Disconnect the wire leading from the coil to the distributor and measure from the coil terminal to ground. If voltage is present, the distributor is shorted. Examine breaker points and connecting wires carefully. If voltage is still not present, measure the other coil terminal. Voltage on the other terminal indicates a defective coil. No voltage indicates a broken wire between the coil and battery.

Weak Spark

If the spark is so small it cannot jump from the wire to ground, check the battery. Other causes are bad breaker points, condenser, incorrect point gap, dirty or loose connection in the primary circuit, or dirty or burned rotor or distributor. Check for worn cam lobes in the distributor.

Missing

This is usually caused by fouled or damaged plugs, plugs of the wrong heat range, or incorrect plug gap.

FUEL SYSTEM TROUBLESHOOTING

Fuel system troubles must be isolated to the carburetor, fuel, pump, or fuel lines. The following procedures assume the ignition system has been checked and is in proper working order.

Engine Will Not Start

First, determine that fuel is being delivered to the carburetor. If fuel is delivered to the carburetor, check the carburetor and choke system for dirt and/or defects.

Engine Runs at Fast Idle

Misadjustment of fast idle screw or defective carburetor.

EXHAUST EMISSION CONTROL TROUBLESHOOTING

Failure of the exhaust emission control system to maintain exhaust emissions within acceptable limits is usually due to defective carburetor, general engine condition, or defective exhaust control valves.

CLUTCH TROUBLESHOOTING

Several clutch troubles may be experienced. Usually the trouble is quite obvious and will fall into one of the following categories:
1. Slipping, chattering, or grabbing when engaging.
2. Spinning or dragging when disengaged.
3. Clutch noises, clutch pedal pulsations, and rapid clutch disc facing wear.

Clutch Slips While Engaged

Improper adjustment of clutch linkage, weak or broken pressure springs, worn friction disc facings, and grease, dirt, or oil on clutch disc.

Clutch Chatters or Grabs When Engaging

Usually caused by misadjustment of clutch linkage, dirt or grease on the clutch disc facings, or broken and/or worn clutch parts.

Clutch Spins or Drags When Disengaged

The clutch disc normally spins briefly after disengagement and takes a moment to come to rest. This sound should not be confused with drag. Drag is caused by the friction disc not being fully released from the flywheel or pressure plate as the clutch pedal is depressed. The trouble can be caused by clutch linkage misadjustment or defective or worn clutch parts.

Clutch Noises

Clutch noises are usually most noticeable when the engine is idling. First, note whether the noise is heard when the clutch is engaged or disengaged. Clutch noises when engaged could be due to a loose friction disc hub, loose friction disc springs, and misalignment or looseness of engine or transmission mountings. When disengaged, noises can be due to a worn release bearing, defective pilot bearing, or misaligned release lever.

Clutch Plate Pulsates

Usually noticed when slight pressure is applied to the clutch pedal with the engine running. As pedal pressure is increased, the pulsation ceases. Possible causes include misalignment of engine and transmission, bent crankshaft flange, distortion or shifting of the clutch housing, release lever misalignment, warped friction disc facing, and damaged pressure plate.

Rapid Friction Disc-Facing Wear

This trouble is caused by any condition that permits slippage between facing and the flywheel or pressure plate. Probable causes are "riding" the clutch, slow releasing of the clutch after disengagement, weak or broken pressure springs, pedal linkage misadjustment, and warped clutch disc or pressure plate.

TRANSMISSION TROUBLESHOOTING

Hard Shifting into Gear

Common causes are the clutch not releasing, misadjustment of linkage, linkage needs lubrication, bent shifter forks, sliding gear tight on shaft splines, sliding gear teeth damaged, and damaged synchronizer.

Transmission Sticks in Gear

May be caused by the clutch not releasing, gearshift linkage out of adjustment, linkage needing lubrication, detent ball stuck, or gears tight on shaft splines.

Transmission Slips Out of First or Reverse Gear

Causes are gearshift linkage out of adjustment, gear loose on mainshaft, gear teeth worn, excessive play, insufficient shift lever spring tension, or worn bearings.

Transmission Slips Out of Second, Third, Fourth, or Fifth Gear

Gearshift linkage is out of adjustment, misalignment between engine and transmission, excessive mainshaft end play, worn gear teeth, insufficient shift-lever spring tension, worn bearings, or defective synchronizer. Gear may be loose on mainshaft.

No Power Through Transmission

May be caused by clutch slipping, stripped gear teeth, damaged shifter fork linkage, broken gear or shaft, and stripped drive key.

Transmission Noisy in Neutral

Transmission misaligned, bearings worn or dry, worn gears, worn or bent countershafts, and excessive countershaft end play.

Transmission Noisy in Gear

Defective clutch disc, worn bearings, loose gears, worn gear teeth, and faults listed above.

Gears Clash During Shifting

Caused by the clutch not releasing, defective hydraulic slave cylinder, defective synchronizer, or gears sticking on mainshaft.

Oil Leaks

Most common causes are foaming due to wrong lubricant, lubricant level too high, broken gaskets, damaged oil seals, loose drain plug, and cracked transmission case.

DIFFERENTIAL/REAR AXLE TROUBLESHOOTING

Usually, it is noise that draws attention to trouble in the differential, rear axle, or driveshaft. It is not always easy to diagnose the trouble by determining the source of noise and the operating conditions that produce the noise. Defective conditions in the universal joints, rear wheel bearings, muffler, or tires may be wrongly diagnosed as trouble in the differential or rear axles.

Some clue as to the cause of trouble may be gained by noting whether the noise is a hum, growl, or knock; whether is it produced when the car is accelerating under load or coasting; and whether it is heard when the car is going straight or making a turn.

Noise During Acceleration—May be caused by shortage of lubricant, incorrect tooth contact between drive gear and drive pinion, damaged or misadjusted bearings in axles or side bearings, or damaged gears.

Noise During Coasting—May be caused by incorrect backlash between drive gear and drive pinion gear or incorrect adjustment of drive pinion bearing.

Noise During Turn—This noise is usually caused by loose or worn axle shaft bearing, pinion gears too tight on shafts, side gear jammed in differential case, or worn side gear thrust washer and pinion thrust washer.

Broken Differential Parts—Breaking of differential parts can be caused by insufficient lubricant, improper use of clutch, excessive loading, misadjusted bearings and gears, excessive backlash, damage to axle case or loose bolts.

Rear Wheel Wobbles—Usually indicates a bent

axle or worn wheel bearings. If wheel bearings, a rumbling noise would probably be heard.

Humming Noise—A humming noise in the differential is often caused by improper drive pinion or ring gear adjustment that prevent normal tooth contact between gears. If ignored, rapid tooth wear will take place and the noise will become more like a growl. Repair as soon as the humming is heard so that new gears will not be required. Tire noise will vary considerably, depending on the type of road surface. Differential noises will be the same regardless of road surface. If noises are heard, listen carefully to the noise over different road surfaces to help isolate the problem.

BRAKE TROUBLESHOOTING

Brake Pedal Goes to Floor

Worn linings or pads, air in the hydraulic system, leaky brake lines, leaky wheel cylinders, or leaky or worn master cylinder may be the cause. Check for leaks and worn brake lining or pads. Bleed and adjust brakes. Rebuild wheel cylinders and/or master cylinder.

Spongy Pedal

Usually caused by air in the brake system. Bleed and adjust brakes.

Brakes Pull

Check brake adjustment and wear on linings and disc pads. Check for contaminated linings, leaky wheel cylinders, loose calipers, lines, or hoses. Check front end alignment and suspension damage such as broken front or rear springs and shock absorbers. Tires also affect braking; check tire pressures and tire condition.

Brakes Squeal or Chatter

Check brake and pad lining thickness and brake drum and rotor condition. Ensure that shoes are not loose. Clean away all dirt on shoes, drums, rotors, and pads.

Brakes Drag

Check brake adjustment, including handbrake. Check for broken or weak shoe return springs, swollen rubber parts due to improper

fluid or contamination. Check for defective master cylinder.

Hard Pedal

Check brake linings for contamination. Check for brake line restrictions.

High Speed Fade

Check for distorted or out-of-round drums and rotors and contaminated linings or pads.

Pulsating Pedal

Check for distorted or out-of-round brake drums or rotors. Check for excessive run-out.

COOLING SYSTEM TROUBLESHOOTING

Engine Overheats

May be caused by insufficient coolant, loose fan belt, defective fan belt, defective thermostat, defective water pump, clogged water lines, incorrect ignition timing, and/or defective or loose hoses. Inspect radiator and all parts for leaks.

Engine Does Not Warm Up

Usually caused by defective thermostat or extremely cold weather.

Loss of Coolant

Radiator leaks, loose or defective hoses, defective water pump, leaks in cylinder head gasket, cracked cylinder head or engine block, or defective radiator cap may be the cause.

Noisy Cooling System

Usually caused by defective water pump bearings, loose or bent fan blades, or defective fan belt.

STEERING AND SUSPENSION TROUBLESHOOTING

Trouble in the suspension or steering is evident when any of the following occur:
1. Hard steering
2. Car pulls to one side
3. Car wanders or front wheels wobble

4. Excessive play in steering

5. Abnormal tire wear

Unusual steering, pulling, or wandering is usually caused by bent or misaligned suspension parts. If the trouble seems to be excessive play, check the wheel bearing adjustment first. Next, check steering free-play and king pins and ball joints. Finally, check tie rod ends by shaking each wheel for signs of looseness.

TIRE WEAR ANALYSIS

Abnormal tire wear should always be analyzed to determine the cause. The most common are incorrect tire pressure, improper driving, overloading, and incorrect wheel alignment.

Figure 2 identifies wear patterns and their most probable causes.

Wheel Balancing

All four wheels and tires must be in balance along two axes. To be in static balance, weight must be evenly distributed around the axis of rotation. **Figure 3**(A) shows a statically unbalanced wheel. Figure 3(B) shows the result — wheel tramp or hopping. Figure 3(C) shows proper static balance.

To be in dynamic balance, the centerline of weight must coincide with the centerline of the wheel. **Figure 4**(A) shows a dynamically unbalanced wheel. Figure 4(B) shows the result — wheel wobble or shimmy. Figure 4(C) shows the proper dynamic balance.

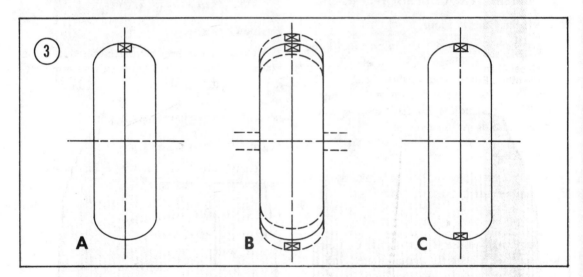

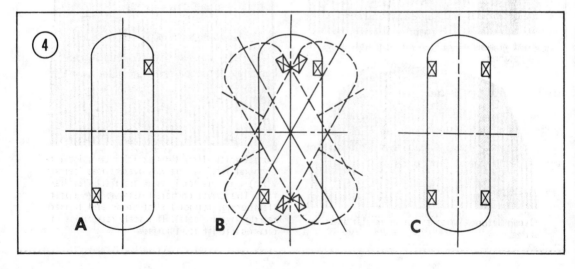

Underinflation—Worn more on sides than in center.

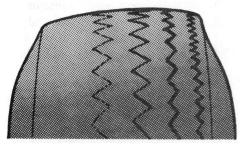

Wheel Alignment—Worn more on one side than the other. Edges of tread feathered.

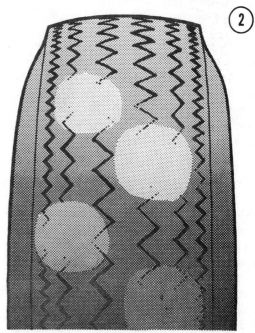

Wheel Balance — Scalloped edges indicate wheel wobble or tramp due to wheel unbalance.

Road Abrasion—Rough wear on entire tire or in patches.

Overinflation—Worn more in center than on sides.

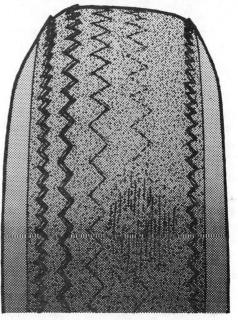

Combination—Most tires exhibit a combination of the above. This tire was overinflated (center worn) and the toe-in was incorrect (feathering). The driver cornered hard at high speed (feathering, rounded shoulders) and braked rapidly (worn spots). The scaly roughness indicates a rough road surface.

CHAPTER FOUR

ENGINE TUNE-UP

The tune-up consists of a series of inspections, adjustments, and parts replacements to compensate for wear and deterioration of engine components. Regular tune-ups are especially important to modern engines. Emission control systems and other factors make these engines especially sensitive to improperly operating or incorrectly adjusted parts.

Since proper engine operation depends upon a number of interrelated system functions, a tune-up consisting of only one or two corrections will seldom get lasting results. A thorough, systematic procedure of analysis and correction will pay dividends in improved power, performance, and operating economy. BMW recommends that the engine be tuned every 8,000 miles (12,500 miles on 1975-1976 models).

GENERAL TUNE-UP PROCEDURES

The procedures presented in this chapter consist of a series of visual and mechanical checks, using the test equipment described in Chapter Three. Tune-up specifications are given in **Table 1**.

The tune-up consists of the following operations, in the order listed:

1. Valve lash adjustment

2. Engine compression check

3. Ignition adjustment and timing, consisting of:

   a. Spark plug replacement

   b. Breaker point replacement and/or adjustment and condenser replacement

   c. Distributor cap and rotor inspection (and replacement, if required)

   d. Spark plug wire inspection (and replacement, if required)

   e. Ignition timing adjustment

4. Carburetor or fuel injection system adjustment

Firing Order

The cylinder firing order for all BMW 1600 and 2002 engines is 1-3-4-2.

CONNECTION OF TUNE-UP EQUIPMENT

Follow the manufacturer's recommendations for the use of test equipment. **Figure 1** is a basic schematic diagram applicable to many types of test equipment and may be used as a guide if the manufacturer's instructions are not available. Connections in Figure 1 are as follows:

Table 1   TUNE-UP SPECIFICATIONS

Engine		Displacement (in. cc)	Transmission	Idle Speed		Compression (in. psi)	Distributor			Spark Plugs			Percent CO
Cylinders	Carburetor ①			Curb	Fast		Point Setting	Dwell Angle	At Engine Speed (rpm)	(Bosch) Type	Gap (Inch)	Timing	
4	38PDSI	1,573 (1,600)	M	700-800	N/A	135-150	4mm (0.016 in.)	59-65°	800	W200T30 WG190T30	0.024-0.028 0.024-0.028	3°BTDC static 25°BTDC @ 1,400 rpm	
4	40PDSIT	1,990 (2,002)	M/A	700-800	N/A	135-150	4mm (0.016 in.)	58-64°	800	W200T30 WG190T30	0.024-0.028 0.024-0.028	3°BTDC static 25°BTDC @ 1,400 rpm	
4	40PHH	1,990 (2,002ti)	M	700-900	N/A	135-150	4mm (0.016 in.)	60°	800	W225T2	0.028	TDC static 25°BTDC @ 2,200 rpm	
4	Kugelfischer injection	1,990 (2,002tii)	M/A	850-950	N/A	135-150	4mm (0.016 in.)	59-65°	900	W175T30	0.024-0.028	TDC static 25°BTDC @ 2,400 rpm	2-3
4	32/32 DIDTA	1,990 (2,002)	M/A	850-950	1,600	135-150	4mm (0.016 in.)	58-64°	900	W200T30 ③ ④	0.024-0.028	TDC static 25°BTDC @ 1,400 ② rpm	0.8-1.2

① Solex unless otherwise noted.
② 25° at 2,800 rpm on 1975-1976 U.S. models.
③ Bosch W175T30 on 1975-1976 U.S. models.
④ Champion N9Y on 1975-1976 U.S. models.

4

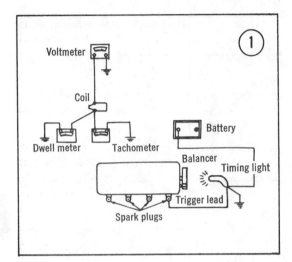

1. Voltmeter
   a. Positive lead to resistor side of coil
   b. Negative lead to ground
2. Timing light
   a. Positive lead to positive battery terminal
   b. Trigger lead to No. 1 spark plug
   c. Negative lead to ground
3. Tachometer
   a. Positive lead to distributor side of coil
   b. Negative lead to ground
4. Dwell meter
   a. Positive lead to distributor side of coil
   b. Negative lead to ground

VALVE CLEARANCE ADJUSTMENT

To check and adjust clearance, proceed as follows. The engine must be cold—having been allowed to stand for several hours or preferably overnight.

1. Remove engine breather connecting hose.

2. Remove bolts, nuts, and washers holding valve cover to top of cylinder head. Take off the valve cover. Take care not to damage valve cover gasket so that it can be re-used. Make certain the ignition lead clip is freed before removing cover.

3. Remove spark plugs to make it easier to rotate crankshaft.

4. Measure the clearance and adjust the valves in firing order; 1-3-4-2. Starting with No. 1 cylinder, rotate the crankshaft until both valves are closed and the piston is at top dead center on the compression stroke.

5. See **Figure 2**. Use a proper size feeler gauge to measure the clearance between the top of the valve and the rocker arm eccentric.

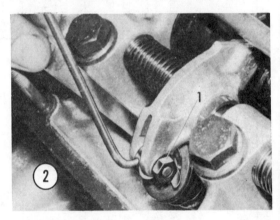

6. If clearance needs adjusting, loosen the locknut (1) on the rocker arm, insert a piece of 0.1 in. (2.5mm) wire in the hole in the eccentric, and rotate the eccentric until the clearance is correct (0.006-0.008 in.). When correct, tighten locknut and recheck clearance.

7. Repeat the above steps for each cylinder.

COMPRESSION TEST

A compression test is performed to check for worn piston rings or to detect the cause of a low-speed miss. Before performing the test, eliminate the possibility of sticky valves by using one of the oil additives designed for the purpose. With valves free, test compression as follows.

1. Run the engine until normal operating temperature is reached.

2. Shut off the engine, remove air cleaner, and block the throttle and choke in the wide open position.

3. Remove spark plugs from cylinder head.

4. Sequentially press a compression test gauge into each of the spark plug holes and crank the engine for at least 4 strokes. Record the compression reading for each cylinder. Normal compression reading is 135-150 psi.

5. No reading should be less than 80% of the highest cylinder reading. Excessive variations between cylinders, accompanied by low speed missing of the cylinder or cylinders usually indicates a valve not properly seating or a broken piston ring.

Low pressures, even though uniform, may indicate worn piston rings. This is especially true if excessive oil consumption has been noticed. If one or more cylinders read low or uneven, inject about a tablespoon of engine oil on top of the piston of that cylinder and crank the engine several times, noting the compression reading. If compression has risen, the piston rings or cylinder walls are worn and should be serviced. If compression does not improve after adding oil, the valves are sticking, burnt, or not seating properly. If 2 adjacent cylinders have low compression, and injecting oil does not increase the reading, the head gasket between the cylinders is probably leaking.

IGNITION
ADJUSTMENT AND TIMING

Spark Plug Inspection and Service

BMW recommends that spark plugs be replaced every 8,000 miles (12,500 miles on 1975-1976 models). This is a good practice. In an emergency, however, plugs in good condition can be cleaned, regapped, and reused. Following is a procedure for inspecting and servicing spark plugs.

1. Remove spark plug wires. Mark them as to the cylinder each is from. Plug condition can give evidence of internal engine problems.

2. Use proper size socket and wrench to remove spark plugs from the cylinder head. Make certain that the gaskets are removed from the spark plug holes.

3. Wipe off the insulator with a clean rag. Remove all grease and dirt.

4. Inspect the insulator and body of each plug for signs of cracks and chips. Replace if faulty.

5. Inspect spark plug threads and electrodes for damage and wear. Replace as required. **Figure 3** shows the condition of normal and defective spark plugs, along with an explanation of the causes of abnormal conditions.

6. If the spark plugs are still serviceable, clean them thoroughly with a stiff brush or, preferably, with a standblasting type of cleaner.

7. File the center electrode flat.

8. Clean and file all surfaces of the outer electrodes. All surfaces should be clean, flat, and smooth.

9. Using a feeler gauge, adjust clearance between electrodes as specified in Table 1. Adjust the gap by bending the outer electrode only. Do not attempt to bend the inner electrode or damage to the insulator may result.

10. Reinstall spark plugs. Make certain to use a new gasket for each plug. Use torque wrench to tighten plugs to 18-22 ft.-lb.

11. Reinstall wires.

Distributor Inspection and Service

Although BMW recommends the replacement of distributor breaker points every 8,000 miles (12,500 miles on 1975-1976 models), points which are still in good condition can be dressed and reused in an emergency. The following procedure covers distributor service.

1. Remove distributor cap. Clean it carefully to remove grease and dirt.

2. Examine the inside of the cap for dirt and wear. Look for signs of carbon tracks (arcing) from contact to contact inside the distributor cap. Carbon tracks indicate defects or cracks. If any are found, replace the cap.

3. Remove the rotor and inspect for excessive wear or burning around the top metal contact surface. If defective, replace. As a matter of good practice, replace the rotor whenever the contact points are replaced.

4. See **Figure 4**. Gently open the contact points with a screwdriver and check their condition. If the points look like No. 1 in the illustration, they are acceptable; if they look like No. 2, they must be replaced. If they show wear or pitting, remove the contact point assembly and clean or replace the points. Use a point file to clean contacts. Do not attempt to remove all roughness.

5. Apply a trace of bearing lubricant to the breaker cam. Saturate the felt in the middle of the rotor shaft with engine oil. Be careful not to get oil in the distributor body.

4

SPARK PLUG CONDITION

③

NORMAL
- Identified by light tan or gray deposits on the firing tip.
- Can be cleaned.

GAP BRIDGED
- Identified by deposit buildup closing gap between electrodes.
- Caused by oil or carbon fouling. If deposits are not excessive, the plug can be cleaned.

OIL FOULED
- Identified by wet black deposits on the insulator shell bore electrodes.
- Caused by excessive oil entering combustion chamber through worn rings and pistons, excessive clearance between valve guides and stems, or worn or loose bearings. Can be cleaned. If engine is not repaired, use a hotter plug.

CARBON FOULED
- Identified by black, dry fluffy carbon deposits on insulator tips, exposed shell surfaces and electrodes.
- Caused by too cold a plug, weak ignition, dirty air cleaner, defective fuel pump, too rich a fuel mixture, improperly operating heat riser, or excessive idling. Can be cleaned.

LEAD FOULED
- Identified by dark gray, black, yellow, or tan deposits or a fused glazed coating on the insulator tip.
- Caused by highly leaded gasoline. Can be cleaned.

WORN
- Identified by severely eroded or worn electrodes.
- Caused by normal wear. Should be replaced.

FUSED SPOT DEPOSIT
- Identified by melted or spotty deposits resembling bubbles or blisters.
- Caused by sudden acceleration. Can be cleaned.

OVERHEATING
- Identified by a white or light gray insulator with small black or gray brown spots and with bluish-burnt appearance of electrodes.
- Caused by engine overheating, wrong type of fuel, loose spark plugs, too hot a plug, low fuel pump pressure, or incorrect ignition timing. Replace the plug.

PREIGNITION
- Identified by melted electrodes and possibly blistered insulator. Metallic deposits on insulator indicate engine damage.
- Caused by wrong type of fuel, incorrect ignition timing or advance, too hot a plug, burned valves, or engine overheating. Replace the plug.

6. Once the points have been cleaned or replaced, install the assembly in the distributor.

7. **Figure 5** shows the breaker point assembly for the 1600 and 2002; **Figure 6** for the 2002ti. Slightly loosen locking screw (a), insert a screwdriver blade between the 2 small studs (b) so that it engages with slot (c) on the contact breaker mounting. Turn the blade gently until the proper gap is set with the use of a feeler gauge, as shown in **Figure 7**. Set the point gap as specified in Table 1. Make certain the rubbing arm on the contact assembly is resting on the high point of the cam. When the gap is correct, tighten screw (a). Recheck gap for accuracy.

8. As a matter of good practice, replace condenser whenever points and rotor are replaced.

9. Inspect the insulation on all wires leading to or within the distributor. Replace if defective.

10. Inspect the wire towers atop the distributor cap for signs of dirt or corrosion. A pencil with fine emery cloth wrapped around the eraser

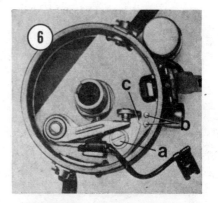

end can be used to clean and burnish the metal surfaces. Make certain to blow out any dust or foreign material.

11. Replace the rotor and cap on the distributor. Firmly insert ignition wires into proper towers in cap.

Dwell Angle Setting

1. Connect dwell angle meter according to instructions.

2. Start the engine and bring to normal operating temperature.

3. See **Figure 8**. Dwell angle S should be as specified in Table 1.

4. If dwell angle is not correct, loosen contact breaker point adjusting screw and adjust breaker points, as previously described.

5. When dwell angle is as specified, tighten adjusting screw.

Spark Plug Wire Inspection

Clean spark plug wires with a cloth immersed in kerosene. Examine for cracked or damaged

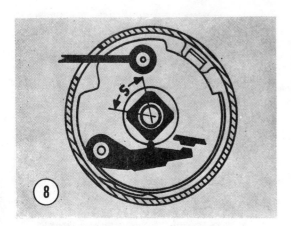

insulation. If engine has been misfiring, check wires for conductor continuity. Make sure all connections are tight and making electrical contact.

Ignition Timing

Ignition timing can be adjusted with the engine running or turned off. The following procedure should be followed when the engine is running. For details on setting the timing with engine turned off, refer to *Static Timing* at the end of this chapter.

1. Make certain spark plug and distributor point gaps are set accurately.

2. Disconnect the vacuum line from the carburetor to the distributor. Plug the end of the vacuum line with tape or stopper.

3. Hook up stroboscopic timing light per instructions provided by the manufacturer.

4. Hook up tachometer per instructions.

5. Start the engine and warm it up to normal operating temperature.

6. See **Figure 9**. The timing mark "Z" (pressed in steel ball) for the No. 1 cylinder is on the flywheel and is visible through the inspection hole in the clutch bell housing, directly above the starter motor.

7. Refer to Table 1 for correct timing figures. Start the engine and set the engine speed with the tachometer by adjusting idle speed with the idle speed adjusting screw, as described in Chapter Seven.

8. Once idle speed is adjusted accurately, aim the timing light at the inspection hole. When the

light flashes, the timing mark should be visible through the hole. Timing is accurate when the center of the ball lines up with the edge of the inspection hole, as shown in Figure 9.

9. If the timing is not accurate, loosen the nut at the base of the distributor and rotate the distributor body until the center of the mark lines up. Tighten the nut.

10. Once timing is correct, shut off the engine, remove the timing light and tachometer, and connect vacuum advance line to distributor.

CARBURETOR ADJUSTMENT

Engine Idle Speed (Early Models)

1. Start the engine and run it until normal operating speed is reached.

2. Adjust ignition timing and valve clearance, as specified in this chapter.

3. (*1600, 2002, 2002A*) See **Figure 10**. Install a tachometer and adjust engine speed to 800 rpm with idle speed adjust screw (1). Tighten or loosen idle speed mixture regulating screw (2) until the engine runs rough. Adjust the idle

speed mixture regulating screw until the engine reaches maximum idling speed and runs smoothly. Adjust the idle speed to 800 rpm. Readjust the idle speed mixture if necessary.

4. (*2002ti*) See **Figure 11**. Turn off the engine. Tighten the 4 idle speed mixture regulating screws (1-4) until tight. Back each screw off 1½ turns. Unscrew synchronizing screw (5) until it no longer contacts the throttle lever. Unscrew idle speed adjusting screw (6) as far as possible. Tighten the synchronizing screw (5) until it just contacts the throttle lever. Screw in the idle speed adjusting screw (6) until contact is made and then tighten up 2 turns.

4

5. (*2002ti*) See **Figure 12**. Connect tachometer, remove air filter, and start engine. Use idle speed mixture regulating screws until engine is running at 1,200 rpm. Use a Unitester (or equivalent) until air flow in all 4 throats is equal. The air flow is correct when the Unitester indicator stays at zero. Adjust carburetor II to coincide with carburetor III with synchronizing screw (5). Adjust carburetor I to coincide with carburetor II with connecting screw (7) shown in **Figure 13**. Adjust carburetor III to coincide with carburetor IV with connecting screw (8) shown in **Figure 14**.

> NOTE: *During adjustment, increase rpm several times so that the spark plugs do not soot up.*

After synchronizing, set the mixture regulating screws (1-4) to the best setting for smooth

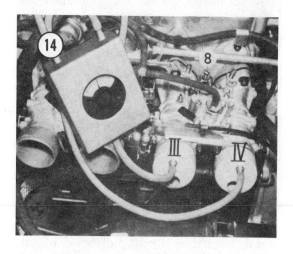

running. See **Figure 15**. Use idle speed setscrew (6) to adjust speed to 800 rpm. If necessary, readjust mixture regulating screws (1-4).

Engine Idle Speed (Late Models Using Solex 32/32 DIDTA Carburetor)

If the car is equipped with the 2-barrel Solex 32/32 DIDTA carburetor, adjust the idle speed by using the following procedure.

1. Connect a tachometer, using the manufacturer's instructions.

2. Turn idle air bypass screw (1, **Figure 16**) to obtain an idle speed of 900 ± 50 rpm.

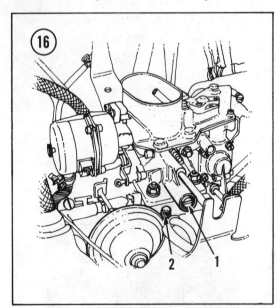

CAUTION
Do not attempt to set idle speed by adjusting the throttle valve stop screw. This setting is made at the factory and must not be changed.

3. Connect an exhaust gas analyzer (one that reads out in percent of carbon monoxide (CO),

using the manufacturer's instructions. Adjust the idle mixture screw (2, Figure 16) to obtain a reading of 0.8-1.2 percent CO. Readjust the idle air bypass screw, if required, to obtain 900 ± 50 rpm.

4. Disconnect the vacuum hose to the carburetor (2, **Figure 17**) and plug hose. Operate the throttle linkage up to approximately 2,500 rpm, then gradually decrease engine speed until setscrew is contacted. Engine speed should be 1,600 ± 50 rpm. If not, adjust to this speed by loosening dashpot locknut and turning dashpot. Tighten locknut.

BATTERY INSPECTION AND SERVICE

1. Check the level of the electrolyte in battery cells. If necessary, replenish with distilled water. The acid level should be just above the upper surface of the plates in each cell, or level with the bar which can be seen through the plug orifice, as shown in **Figure 18**.

2. Measure the specific gravity of the battery electrolyte with hydrometer. Refer to **Table 2**.

Table 2   ELECTROLYTE SPECIFIC GRAVITY

	Permissible Value	Full Charge Value (68°F., 20°C.)
Moderate climates	Over 1.20	1.26
Frigid climates	Over 1.22	1.28
Tropical climates	Over 1.18	1.23

3. Clean top of battery and terminals with a solution of baking soda and water. Rinse off and dry thoroughly.

4. Tighten cable connectors to the terminals securely.

5. Coat the terminals lightly with Vaseline to protect them from corrosion.

ADDITIONAL CHECKS

During tune-ups, check the following items for signs of defects or wear.

1. Inspect carburetor for buildup of foreign material. Pay special attention to carburetor throat and linkages.

2. Check all belts, hoses, and fuel lines. **Repair** or replace as required. Check the belt tension on the water pump and generator (alternator). See **Figure 19**. Normal belt deflection when pushed in under thumb pressure should be approximately 0.4 in. (10mm).

3. Inspect oil filter for leaks. Tighten or replace as necessary.

4. Inspect the air cleaner for dirt. Replace as required.

5. Inspect water pump, radiator, and associated hoses of leaks. Repair or replace if defective.

6. Check emission control device. Refer to Chapter Ten.

7. Check engine oil. Replenish or replace as required.

8. Check the fluid level in the brake and clutch master cylinders. Replenish as necessary.

9. Examine the condition of windshield wipers. Replace if defective.

STATIC IGNITION TIMING

This procedure is performed with the engine off and cold (under 95°F). It may be used on older models if a stroboscopic timing light is not available, or in an emergency on later models, if equipped with timing marks as described in Step 3.

1. Connect a 12-volt test light between the No. 1 terminal on the ignition coil and ground.

2. Remove the high tension lead between the coil and the distributor, and turn on the ignition.

3. Using a metric socket wrench and extension, apply torque to the crankshaft pulley nut and turn the engine clockwise. The lamp should light as soon as the notch or mark on the crankshaft pulley lines up with the pointer on the engine block. See **Figures 20 and 21**.

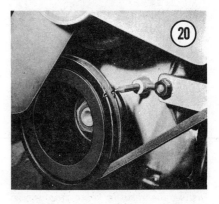

4. If required, loosen the distributor clamp nut (**Figure 22**) and adjust by turning the distributor body (clockwise to retard, counterclockwise to advance). Retighten the clamp nut.

NOTE: *The test lamp should light at the instant the pointer becomes aligned with the notch. If more than one notch is present, see Table 1 for specification for your engine.*

5. Recheck the setting by turning the crankshaft about 45 degrees counterclockwise, at which point the test lamp should go out. Then turn clockwise until the pointer and notch are aligned, at which point the lamp should come on again. Readjust and recheck, if necessary.

CHAPTER FIVE

ENGINE

This chapter provides information and procedures for engine removal, disassembly, repair, replacement, reassembly, and installation.

Except for differences in bore, stroke, and carburetion, the different engines are virtually the same. Procedures given in this chapter generally apply to all models, with exceptions noted.

Figure 1 is a cutaway view of the 1600 and 2002, **Figure 2** the 2002 ti, and **Figure 3** the 2002tii. The engines feature 4 inline cylinders and a single overhead camshaft for valve operation. The crankshaft is supported by 5 replaceable shell-type bearings. The connecting rod bearings are also replaceable shell types. The crankshaft, through pulleys, sprockets, and chains, drives the water pump, oil pump, generator (alternator), camshaft, emission control air pump, and the fuel injection pump (if so equipped). The distributor and fuel pump are driven by camshaft lobes and gearing.

The 1600 and early 2002 are fitted with a single throated carburetor. (Solex 38 PDSI and 40 PDSI, typically). Later 2002's are fitted with a Solex 32/32 DIDTA 2-barrel with automatic choke. The 2002ti has 2 dual, side-draft carburetors, and the 2002tii is fitted with a fuel injection system. Details on the carburetors are given in Chapter Seven.

SERVICE HINTS

Removal of the crankshaft from the block is the only operation which dictates engine removal from the car. If major work is to be done, however, it will be easier if the engine is on a bench or stand rather than in the car.

It is easier to work on a clean engine than a dirty one, and you will do a better job. Before starting, have the engine and under-chassis steam cleaned or clean them with a good commercial degreaser, following the manufacturer's instructions. Make certain you have the necessary tools available and a clean place in which to work.

It is a good idea to identify and mark parts as they are removed so that errors will be avoided during assembly and installation. Make certain all parts related to a particular cylinder, piston connecting rod, and/or valve assembly are identified for replacement in the proper place. Do not rely too heavily on your memory; it may be days or weeks before you complete the job.

Detailed specifications, clearances, and torque tightening information are given in **Table 1** at the end of this chapter. Use and comply with this information. If a part is marginal according to specification, repair or replace it so that your work will not be wasted.

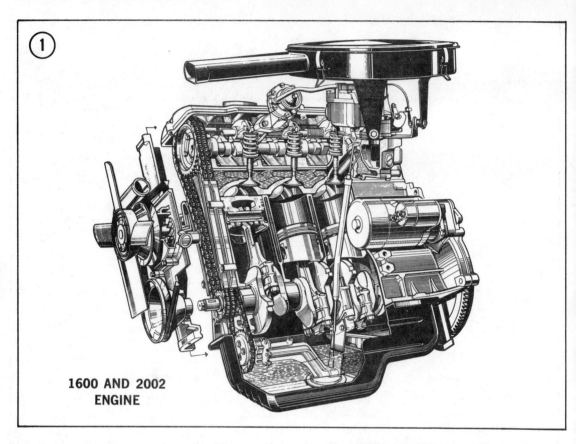

① 1600 AND 2002 ENGINE

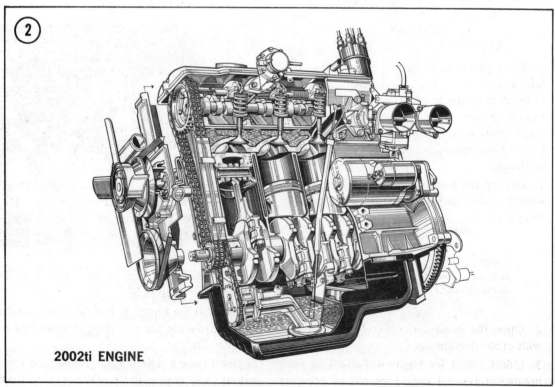

② 2002ti ENGINE

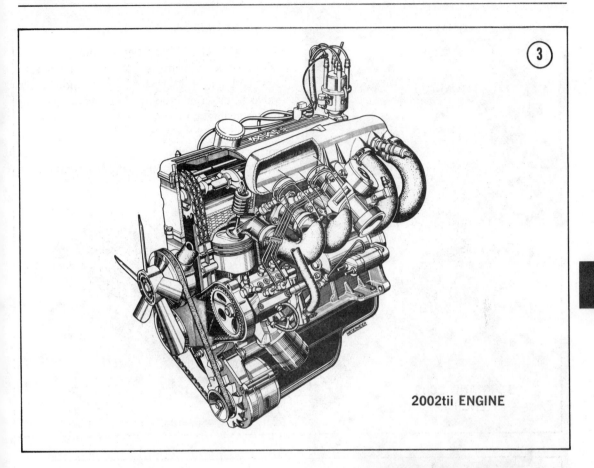

2002tii ENGINE

ENGINE REMOVAL/REPLACEMENT

Before proceeding, read all instructions carefully and study the illustrations so that you have in mind the steps to be taken. Removal of the engine should only be necessary to perform major overhaul of the block and its associated parts. Other repairs can be done with the engine in place.

1. Jack up the front of the car and support it securely with jackstands or sturdy wooden blocks.

WARNING
Never get under a car supported by a jack only. Should the jack fall, injury or death could result.

2. Open the hood and cover fender surfaces with protective aprons.

3. (*1600, 2002*) See **Figure 4**. Pull off air filter breather tube and connector out of breather

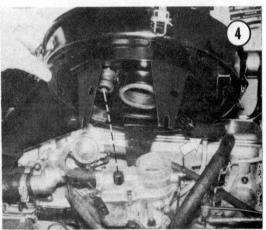

tube. Disassemble and remove air filter, as described in Chapter Six.

4. (*2002ti*) See **Figure 5**. Pull off breather tube and disassemble the air filter, as described in Chapter Six.

5. See **Figure 6**. Disconnect ground lead from battery and engine block. Detach plug from

7. Remove the radiator (Chapter Eight).

8. Disconnect fuel line from fuel pump. Pull off wire connector from remote thermometer sensor. Disconnect vacuum line with non-return valve from screw union and hot water hose for heater at intake manifold.

9. (*1600, 2002*) See **Figure 8**. Detach return spring (1) and clamp spring (2). Disconnect control rod (3) and pull out from support on bulkhead.

10. (*2002ti, 2002tii*) Disconnect accelerator-to-carburetor (fuel injection) linkage.

11. (*1600, 2002*) Loosen clamp screw (1) from clamp (2) and pull out the choke cable, as shown in **Figure 9**.

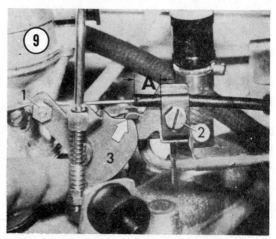

alternator and B+ cable from alternator and starter cable.

6. (*2002A*) See **Figure 7**. Disconnect cable from automatic choke and thermo-start valve. Detach plug from starter lock and pull cable loom out of retainer at transmission.

12. (*2002ti*) See **Figure 10**. Detach return spring (1) and pull rod (2). Lift out the retainer (3) from torsion shaft on carburetor. Pull

torsion shaft toward bulkhead until ball is free of torsion shaft. Remove the torsion shaft toward the front.

13. (*2002A*) See **Figure 11**. Detach the clamp spring (1) and the return spring (2). Lift out wire retainer (3). Pull torsion shaft toward bulkhead until ball is free of torsion shaft. Remove the torsion shaft toward the front.

14. Remove wire connector from oil pressure switch and from distributor at terminal No. 1. Remove distributor cap and pull cable No. 4 off. Remove distributor rotor. Remove hot water hose from cylinder head. See **Figure 12**.

15. See **Figure 13**. Detach pull rod on intermediate shaft. Detach bearing support from engine support. Remove intermediate shaft and pushrod.

16. Loosen and remove nut from left-hand motor mount, as shown in **Figure 14**.

17. Remove the selector lever, as described in Chapter Ten.

18. See **Figure 15**. Remove bolts holding retaining plate (1), support (2), and bracket (3) from exhaust pipe. Disconnect exhaust pipe from exhaust manifold.

19. See **Figure 16**. Disconnect drive shaft from transmission, as described in Chapter Eleven.

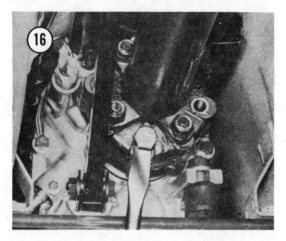

20. Loosen bolts at drive shaft center bearing, as shown in **Figure 17**.

21. See **Figure 18**. Attach an engine hoist with chains, as shown.

22. See **Figure 19**. Remove bolts holding cross-member and remove crossmember. Unscrew speedometer shaft clamp screw and remove speedometer shaft. Remove wire from reverse light switch. On 2002A, detach cable from reverse light connector, and pull off starter lock cable from reverse light/starter lock switch, as shown in Figure 19.

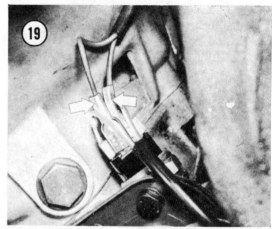

23. Loosen right-hand motor mount, as shown in **Figure 20**. Remove nut. Detach and remove windshield washer water reservoir.

24. Carefully inspect the engine compartment to make certain that all hoses, lines, linkages, and wires have been disconnected from the engine and transmission.

25. Slowly lower the transmission and lift the engine out of the engine compartment over the right fender, as shown in **Figure 21**. Place the engine on a workbench or install it on an engine stand.

26. After engine removal and if the engine is to be completely disassembled, remove transmission, generator, water pump, oil sump, oil pump, carburetor(s), starter motor, and distributor as discussed in other chapters.

27. To replace the engine, reverse the order of the above steps. When recoupling the engine to the transmission, the clutch shaft must be carefully aligned and inserted in the spline slots in the driven clutch plate.

ENGINE SERVICING

The following sections deal with repair and reconditioning of the main engine assemblies including the cylinder block, cylinder head, timing gearing, crankshaft, flywheel, connecting rods, pistons, camshaft, valves, and manifolds.

Since repair and reconditioning techniques generally apply to all internal combustion engines, the discussion below applies specifically to the 1600 and 2002 models. Important dif-

ferences for other models are noted or discussed as required. The specifications, tolerances, and torque tightening information given at the end of this chapter should be followed for your particular engine.

Remove all traces of old gasket material from joint faces with a scraper or electric drill fitted with a wire brush. Make certain that all engine parts are clean and free from damage or defects. Clean and degrease parts in a suitable solvent.

If possible, have the block and cylinder "hot tanked" to clean out oil and water passages. At any rate, pay special attention to the passages to make certain they are not clogged. Check all parts and wear surfaces carefully for conformity with specifications and wear tolerances.

When rebuilding or repairing an engine, always use new gaskets and lock plates. Replace damaged studs, nuts, bolts, spring washers, and leaking core plugs. Use a good quality gasket and joining compound on gaskets, joints, and sealing block faces. The compound should be used according to manufacturer's instructions. Tighten all nuts, bolts, and studs to the correct torque with an accurate torque wrench.

CYLINDER HEAD SERVICING

Servicing of the cylinder head and valves include:

1. Cleaning and decarbonizing.

2. Inspecting all parts for damage and specification compliance.

3. Repairing or reconditioning as required.

The following procedures can be performed with the engine installed or removed from the car. Unless otherwise noted, installation is the reverse of the steps used during removal and disassembly.

Cylinder Head Removal

1. See **Figure 22**. Remove air filter. Disconnect breather tube from cylinder head cover. Loosen and remove 7 nuts holding cylinder head cover to cylinder head. Remove cover. Take care not to damage gasket between cover and cylinder head.

2. Disconnect carburetor linkages as described above under *Engine Removal*.

3. Disconnect water hoses, fuel lines, wiring, and distributor connections as previously described.

4. Remove high tension wires from spark plugs. Mark wires for later replacement. Unscrew and remove spark plugs. Remove distributor cap and spark plug wires.

5. See **Figure 23**. Remove nuts holding timing gear cover to cylinder head and block. Remove the cover.

6. Turn the crankshaft until No. 1 cylinder is at TDC. In this position, both valves on No. 1 cylinder should be closed, and the distributor and pulley timing marks should be aligned, as shown in **Figure 24**.

7. See **Figure 25**. Unscrew and remove the plug and spring holding piston against chain tensioner. Remove the plug carefully because of the spring tension.

8. See **Figure 26**. Push down lock plate ends, loosen and remove 4 fixing bolts, and remove

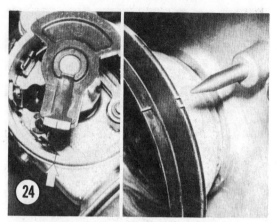

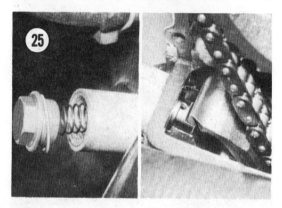

sprocket from mounting flange. Disconnect chain from sprocket. During installation, fit the chain so that the hole for the set pin faces downward. The notch in the camshaft flange must be in alignment with the cast-in projection on the cylinder head, as shown in **Figure 27**.

9. Remove exhaust support and disconnect exhaust pipe from exhaust manifold, as previously described.

10. See **Figure 28**. Remove the 10 cylinder head bolts securing cylinder head to cylinder block. Remove cylinder head and gasket. During installation, tighten the bolts in the sequence shown in the figure to the proper torque. Tighten the bolts gradually until the proper torque is reached. Always use a new head gasket. **Figure 29** is an exploded diagram of the cylinder head and associated parts.

Cylinder Head Decarbonizing

Removal of carbon from combustion chambers and valves should be done with the valves installed in the head. By doing so, damage to valve guides and seats will be avoided.

1. Remove all traces of carbon build-up with a scraper and wire brush fitted to an electric drill.

2. Remove valves from head as discussed below.

3. Polish combustion chambers and ports with fine emery cloth. Be certain to clean head thoroughly after this operation to prevent abrasive material from entering the engine.

Camshaft Removal

Figure 30 is an exploded diagram of the camshaft, rocker arm, and valve assemblies. A special holding fixture, as shown in **Figure 31**, is required to disassemble and assemble the camshaft and valve assemblies. For this reason, it is recommended that servicing procedures be referred to a BMW dealer. If this is not possible, disassembly can be eased by releasing all spring and valve pressure against the camshaft by slackening the rocker arm adjusters and then gradually disassembling the rocker arm assemblies. Once the rocker arms are apart, remove the camshaft as follows.

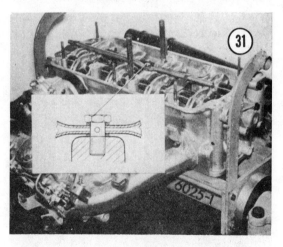

1. Remove camshaft sprocket.

2. Remove rocker arms from cylinder head.

3. Remove fuel pump, as discussed in Chapter Six. Partly pull out the plunger, as shown in **Figure 32**. Loosen clamp screw and remove distributor, as discussed in Chapter Nine. Disconnect oil pipe.

4. With a feeler gauge, check the axial clearance between the camshaft guide plate and camshaft, as shown in **Figure 33**. If clearance is excessive, the camshaft should be replaced. See p. 70

5. Remove 2 bolts holding guide plate to cylinder head. Remove guide plate and carefully withdraw camshaft from cylinder head.

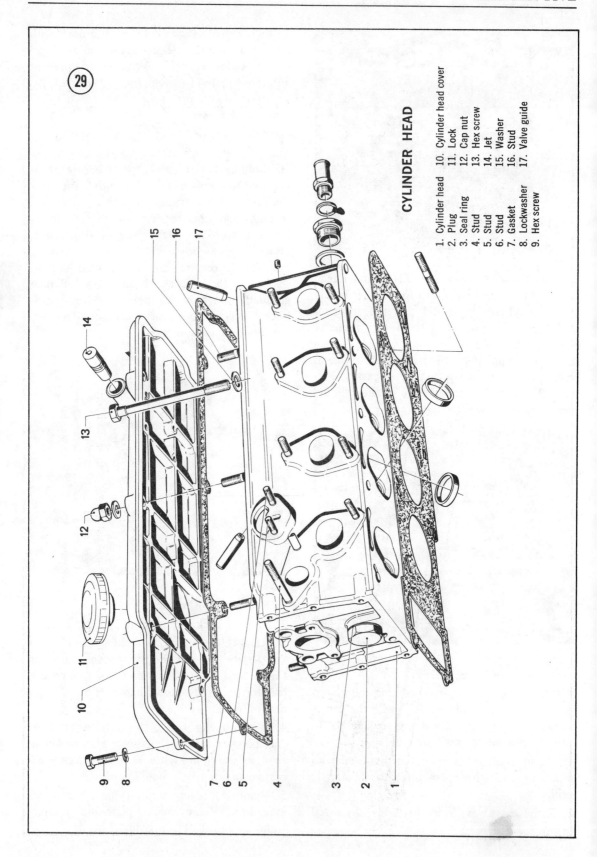

CYLINDER HEAD

1. Cylinder head
2. Plug
3. Seal ring
4. Stud
5. Stud
6. Stud
7. Gasket
8. Lockwasher
9. Hex screw
10. Cylinder head cover
11. Lock
12. Cap nut
13. Hex screw
14. Jet
15. Washer
16. Stud
17. Valve guide

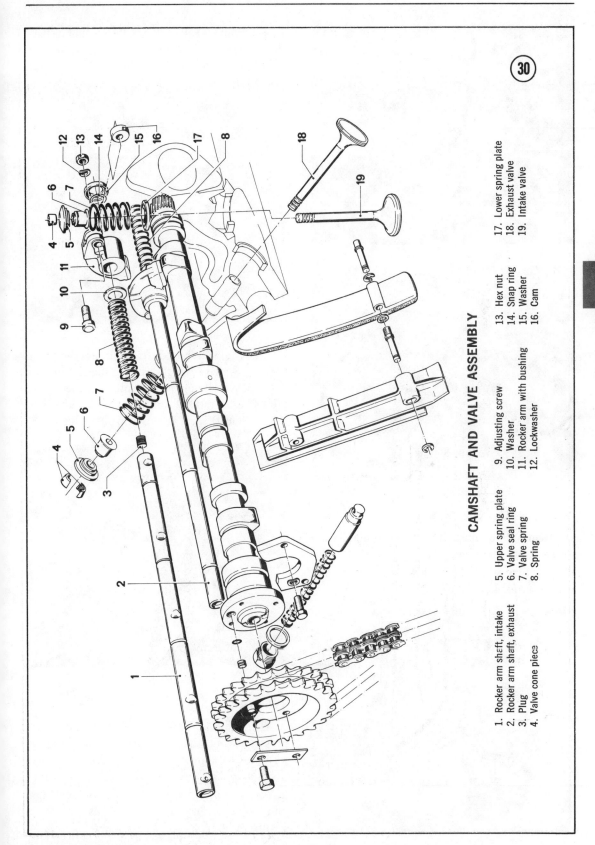

CAMSHAFT AND VALVE ASSEMBLY

1. Rocker arm shaft, intake
2. Rocker arm shaft, exhaust
3. Plug
4. Valve cone piece

5. Upper spring plate
6. Valve seal ring
7. Valve spring
8. Spring

9. Adjusting screw
10. Washer
11. Rocker arm with bushing
12. Lockwasher

13. Hex nut
14. Snap ring
15. Washer
16. Cam

17. Lower spring plate
18. Exhaust valve
19. Intake valve

5

Rocker Shafts/Arms Removal

1. Remove the camshaft by using special fixture 6025-1, or equivalent.

2. See **Figure 34**. Push back thrust rings and rocker arms. Lift out circlips (1).

3. See **Figure 35**. Remove bolts holding distributor flange to head. During assembly, replace self-sealing washers (1) and seals (2) with new ones.

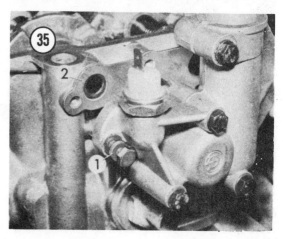

4. Using a suitable drift, such as shown in **Figure 36**, drive out the rocker shafts from the rear of the cylinder head. Note that the end of the left side (intake) shaft is open and the right side (exhaust) shaft is closed with a plug.

Valve Removal

1. Using special fixture 6025-1 or equivalent, press down on the upper spring plate, and remove valve cones from around end of valve. See **Figure 37**.

2. Remove upper spring plate, valve seal ring, and valve spring from valve, as shown in Figure 30.

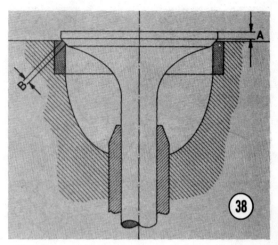

3. Push valve out through bottom of cylinder head. Take care not to damage valve seats or valve seal rings, or excessive oil consumption will result. Mark all parts as they are removed to simplify later replacement in the correct sequence and position.

Cylinder Head Inspection

1. After cleaning and decarbonizing, check head carefully for signs of damage, such as cracks and defective core plugs. If cracked, the head can sometimes be welded satisfactorily. Refer such service to an automotive machine shop. Replace core plugs if they show any signs of rust, leaks, or weakness.

2. Use a long straightedge and thin feeler gauge to check head and block mating surfaces. The surfaces must be flat to prevent leaks. If high spots are found, they can sometimes be eliminated with a scraper. If the cylinder head is distorted, have it resurfaced with a surface grinder. Refer this service to an automotive machine shop.

Valve Servicing

1. Clean valves with a wire brush and solvent. Discard burned, warped, or cracked valves. Check critical valve dimensions against specifications. See **Figure 38** for critical dimensions to be measured. Dimension A is the minimum edge thickness and B the valve seat angle.

2. Remove all carbon and varnish from valve guides with a stiff spiral brush.

3. Insert valve into corresponding valve guide. Hold the face of the valve about ⅛ in. from the valve seat and rock it sideways. Movement of the valve head across the seat must not exceed 0.0013 in. (0.03mm). Check the movement with a dial gauge. If movement is excessive, the valve guide and valve should be replaced with new, standard parts.

4. Measure valve spring heights. Free length of spring should be 1.7126 in. (43.5mm). If springs are weak or distorted, replace with new ones.

5. Check the valve seats for scores, burns, and ridges. If the valve seats will not clean up easily by normal valve-to-seat lapping or if new guides have been fitted, replace the valve seats. Replacement requires removal of the old seat (insert), heating the head and installation of new seat, and grinding to proper angle. Refer such service to your dealer.

6. Grind the valves in their respective seats in the cylinder head either by hand lapping or with a machine such as that shown in **Figure 39**. If hand lapping is to be done, put a light spring under the head and use medium-grade grinding paste. If the seats are in good condition, fine-grade paste may be used. Use a suction cup tool to hold the valve head. Grind with a semi-rotary motion and let the valve rise off the seat occasionally. Use grinding paste sparingly and when pitting has been removed, clean away paste. Use fine-grade paste until valve seat has an even gray finish. Clean away all traces of grinding paste from the valves and ports.

7. Check the valve guides for wear and damage. If the valve guides are defective or if the valve seats are replaced, replace the valve guides.

8. Use a suitable drift, as shown in **Figure 40**, to press the valve guide through the head and out the combustion chamber. Heat the head to approximately 450°F and use a suitable tool, such as shown in **Figure 41**, to install valve guide. Dimension A should be 0.59 in. (15mm). After installation, ream out valve guide to standard dimension.

Camshaft and Journal Servicing

The camshaft journal and cam faces should be perfectly smooth and in good condition. If this is not the case and there are signs of seizing or scoring that cannot be removed with a very fine abrasive stone, the camshaft must be replaced. Journal damage requires replacement of the head.

Inspect the distributor drive gear. If teeth are damaged or badly worn, replace camshaft.

TIMING CHAIN/TENSIONER/ SPROCKET SERVICING

Chain Tensioner Removal/Servicing

1. Remove cylinder head cover and front cover, as previously described.

2. See Figure 25. Unscrew closure plug. Be careful while removing due to the spring pressure. Remove the spring and piston from the housing.

3. See **Figure 42**. Check the length of the piston and spring. Piston length (A) should be 2.441 in. (62mm) and spring length should be 6.122 in. (155.5mm). If either part is defective, replace with a new one.

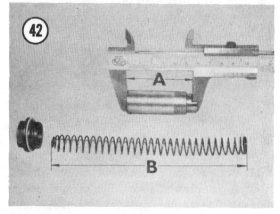

4. See **Figure 43**. Using compressed air, check to see that the bleed slots (1) are not obstructed.

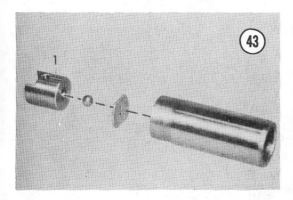

If they are, press out the piston and clean the slots. During assembly, do not cover bleed slots with perforated disc.

5. After installation of the piston and spring into the housing, the piston must be bled. Screw in the plug slightly and fill oil pocket with engine oil. See **Figure 44**. With a screwdriver, move the tension rail backward and forward until oil comes out at the closure plug. Tighten closure plug.

Timing Chain Removal/Servicing

Figure 45 shows the details of the timing chain and associated parts.

1. Remove cylinder head, oil sump, and water pump as discussed in this or other chapters. Unscrew the bolts holding upper gear cover cylinder head. **Figure 46** shows the details of the upper and lower gear covers and gaskets.

2. Loosen cover and lock flywheel with screwdriver, as shown in **Figure 47**.

3. Remove nut holding crankshaft belt pulley to crankshaft and remove belt pulley, as shown

in **Figure 48**. Remove Woodruff key from crankshaft.

5

4. See **Figure 49**. Remove bolts holding alternator to engine and remove alternator.

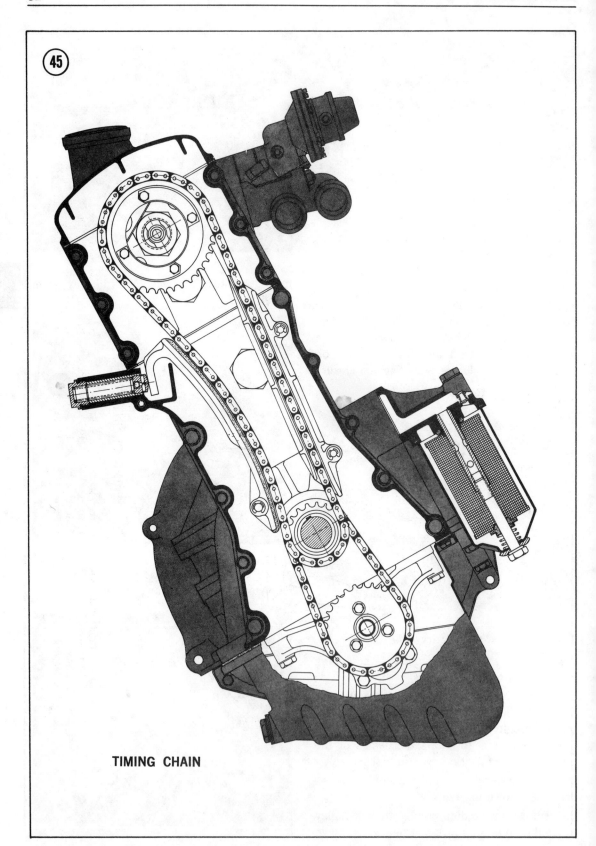

TIMING CHAIN

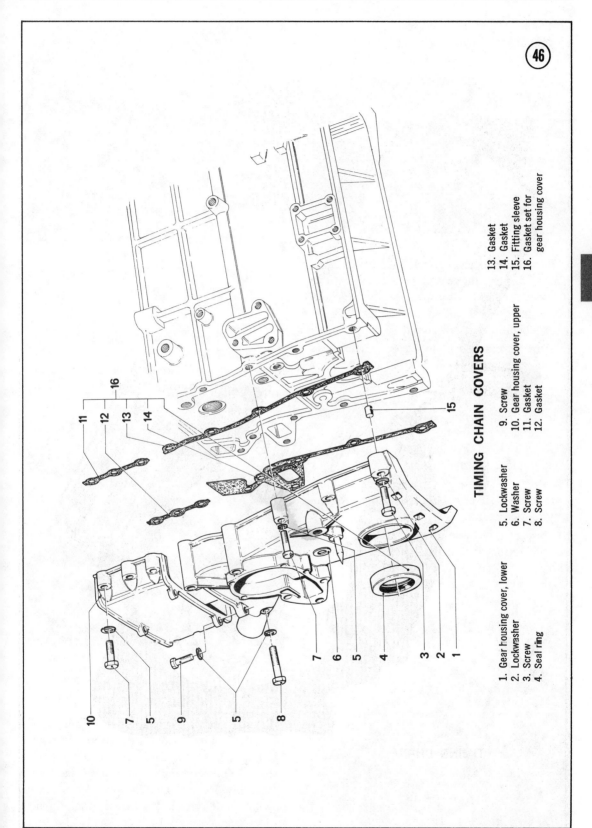

TIMING CHAIN COVERS

1. Gear housing cover, lower
2. Lockwasher
3. Screw
4. Seal ring
5. Lockwasher
6. Washer
7. Screw
8. Screw
9. Screw
10. Gear housing cover, upper
11. Gasket
12. Gasket
13. Gasket
14. Gasket
15. Fitting sleeve
16. Gasket set for gear housing cover

46

5

5. Remove bolts holding lower gear cover in position. Remove cover and gaskets. See **Figure 50**.

6. Inspect the cover and seal ring for wear and damage. Replace the seal ring if defective. If the pulley hub is damaged or severely worn, replace it or install the seal ring so that the seal lip is in front or behind the worn groove.

7. Turn the crankshaft until No. 1 cylinder is at TDC on the compression stroke.

8. Mark the position of the timing chain relative to the location of the crankshaft and camshaft sprockets. Remove plug, spring, and piston from chain tensioner housing. Move the chain tensioner away from the chain so that the chain is slack. Remove the chain from the camshaft and crankshaft sprockets.

9. Inspect all parts for wear and damage. Repair is by replacement.

10. Inspect the condition of the tensioner rail and sliding rail. If wear is excessive, they must be replaced. See **Figures 51 and 52**. Lift out the retainers (1), (2), and (3) and remove the rails.

11. Inspect the condition of the crankshaft drive sprocket. If damaged, replace. See **Figure 53**. Remove bolts holding oil pump, drive sprocket and remove drive sprocket and chain. Remove the Woodruff key (1) and O-ring from crankshaft. Pull off the drive sprocket from the crankshaft. During reassembly, always replace the O-ring with a new one. **Figure 54** shows the drive sprocket being pulled off.

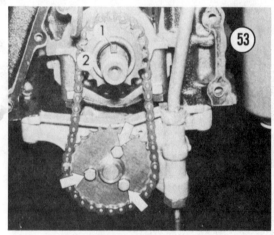

CYLINDER BLOCK SERVICING

Cylinder block reconditioning requires removing the block from car, dismantling and cleaning it, inspecting and replacing worn parts, checking and reboring block as necessary, and reassembly. Remove and disassemble engine as previously described. Procedures that do not require engine removal are so noted.

Measuring Cylinder Bore

Cylinder bore can be measured with the engine in the car. Proceed as follows:

1. Remove cylinder head from cylinder block.

2. See **Figure 55**. Use a cylinder gauge to measure cylinder bore. Take several readings at different locations. Determine the maximum bore wear, which normally occurs toward the top of the bore across the connecting rod thrust axis.

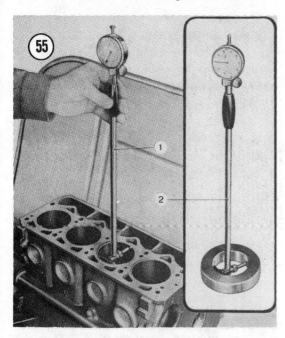

1. Dial gauge	2. Setting gauge to zero with ring gauge A.96136

3. Check readings against wear limit specifications. If wear limit has been exceeded, rebore the block and install oversize rings on the pistons. If wear limit has not been exceeded, hone the cylinders to remove the glaze and to give a good surface for the rings to seat against.

> NOTE: *Reboring of the block requires equipment not normally available to the home mechanic. Refer such service to a dealer or automotive machine shop.*

CONNECTING RODS

Removal of the connecting rods can be done with the engine in place if the oil sump is removed. Normally, however, the engine should be removed. Whenever removal of the connecting rods is required, service the cylinder head, pistons, rings, cylinder bore, bearings, and crankshaft.

Oil Sump Removal/Installation

1. Run the engine until normal operating temperature is reached and drain oil, as previously described.

2. Raise the car on a hoist or jack it up and place the front end on jackstands.

3. *(2000, ti, tii)* Remove the front stabilizer bar, as discussed in Chapter Twelve.

4. Remove nuts and washers holding oil sump to crankcase.

5. Lower sump. Be careful not to damage sump gasket.

6. Loosen left- and right-side engine mountings, as described in *Engine Removal/Replacement* above.

7. See **Figure 56**. Attach chain hoist to engine, as shown.

8. Turn crankshaft until No. 4 piston is at TDC.

9. Lift up the engine slightly until the sump can be removed forward, as shown in **Figure 57**.

10. Use a suitable solvent to clean the sump. Make certain to remove all traces of gasket or gasket sealing compound from the sump and the crankcase mating surfaces.

11. Inspect the sump carefully for cracks and dents. Repair by welding or replace as required.

12. To install, reverse the above procedures. During installation coat all mating surfaces with

5

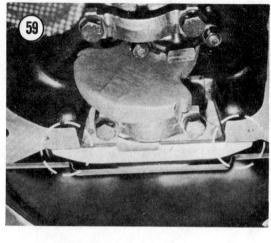

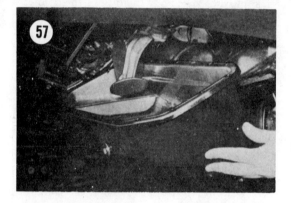

3. Remove rod bearings caps and bearings from crankshaft. Inspect cylinder bore for ridge at top of bore. Use ridge reamer to remove ridge.

4. With ridge removed, push connecting rod and piston assembly out of top of cylinder.

5. Be sure to mark components as to the cylinder or rod from which they were taken.

Piston Pin Removal

Figure 60 shows the details of the connecting rod/piston assemblies. The piston pin (gudgeon pin) is a slip fit to the connecting rod and is held in place in the piston with circlips.

1. With circlip pliers remove circlips at the ends of the piston pin. Separate the piston from the connecting rod.

2. Slide the pin out of the connecting rod, as shown in **Figure 61**.

a suitable gasket compound. Be certain to coat the mating surfaces on the timing gear cover and the end cover, as shown in **Figures 58 and 59**.

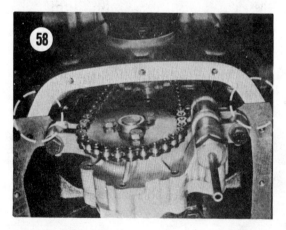

Piston Removal

1. Remove cylinder head.
2. Remove oil sump.

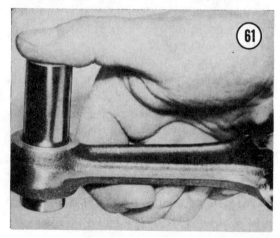

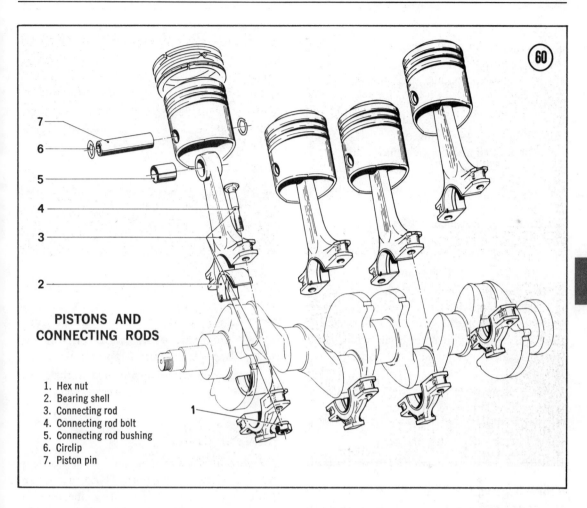

PISTONS AND
CONNECTING RODS

60

7
6
5
4
3
2
1

1. Hex nut
2. Bearing shell
3. Connecting rod
4. Connecting rod bolt
5. Connecting rod bushing
6. Circlip
7. Piston pin

Connecting Rod Inspection/Repair

1. Carefully inspect small end for general condition, scratches, and wear. If defective, replace.

2. If the piston pin is loose in the small end when installed, press out the bushing and press in a new one. When pressing in the new bushing, make certain to offset the abutting ends 90° away from the oil bore in the connecting rod, as shown in **Figure 62**.

3. Have your dealer check the alignment of the connecting rod. If replacement is required, make certain to replace with a rod that has the same color spots marked on it as the old one had. The color spots identify weight class.

PISTONS, PISTON PINS, AND PISTON RINGS

The piston assembly consists of the connecting rod, piston pin, piston rings, and piston. Re-

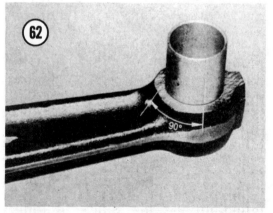

62

90°

moval of this assembly is as described for connecting rods.

Inspection and Repair

1. Use a ring expander to remove rings from pistons. Mark rings for later replacement. It is

recommended that new rings be installed depending on overall engine condition.

2. Inspect all parts for wear and damage. Replace or recondition as required.

3. Remove all carbon from piston with a scraper or broken hacksaw blade. Clean out the ring grooves with a broken ring or groove cleaning tool. The tool should be the same width as the groove being cleaned.

4. Clean out oilways inside piston and connecting rod.

5. Check the clearance between the cylinder bore and piston as shown in Figure 62. Clearance between the piston and cylinder bore should be 0.0015 in. (0.040mm).

6. To check the clearance between the piston and pin, lubricate the pin with clean engine oil and insert it in the piston. If the clearance is correct, the pin should enter easily with thumb pressure and should not slide out under its own weight.

7. Use a feeler gauge to measure the clearance between the rings and grooves, as shown in **Figure 63**. Clearances should be as specified in Table 1 at the end of this chapter.

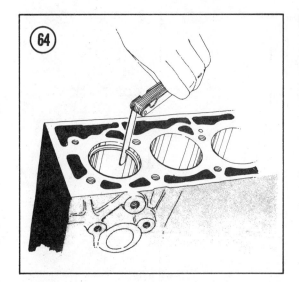

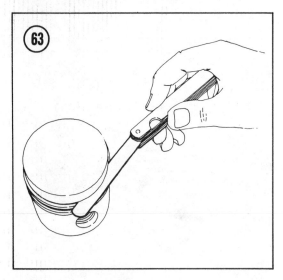

8. Use a feeler gauge to measure the end gap of each ring when installed in cylinder, as shown in **Figure 64**. Check measurement against specification. Replace with new rings as required.

9. Install rings on pistons with ring expander. See **Figure 65**.

Installation

1. Lubricate each piston with clean engine oil. Coat piston rings well.

2. Position the piston rings so that the gaps are staggered 180° from each other and so that none lines up with the thrust side of the piston.

3. Use a piston ring compressor to compress the rings into the piston grooves.

4. Carefully lower the piston assembly into the cylinder bore. Make certain that each piston is inserted into its proper bore and that the arrow on top of the piston faces toward the front of the engine.

> **CAUTION**
> *When installing the piston assembly into the block be careful not to damage or scratch crankshaft bearing journal.*

5. When the bottom of the ring compressor is flat against the top of the block, push on the top of the piston until it is free of the compressor and the rings are in contact with the cylinder walls.

6. Insert connecting rod bearing into connecting rod. Make certain that locating tabs mate with recesses in connecting rod. Lubricate bearing with a light coating of engine oil.

7. Insert big end bearing into connecting rod cap. Lubricate bearing with oil.

8. Install cap to crankshaft, insert rod cap bolts, and tighten to specified torque.

9. Repeat above steps for each piston.

CONNECTING ROD BEARINGS

Inspection/Replacement

1. Inspect the upper and lower half of the connecting rod bearings for signs of scratches or general wear. Do not scrape the bearings or attempt to polish them. If they are defective, replace them.

2. If the bearings appear to be serviceable, measure the clearance between them and the crankshaft journals with Plastigage, or equivalent. To check the clearance, fit the connecting rod/piston assembly to the crankshaft journal, place a piece of Plastigage across the bottom bearing, install the big end cap, and torque tighten to specification.

3. Remove the cap and measure the amount of crushing of the Plastigage by comparing its width to the scale on the envelope, as shown in **Figure 66**. If the clearance is within the tolerance of 0.0009 to 0.0027 in. (0.023 to 0.069mm), it

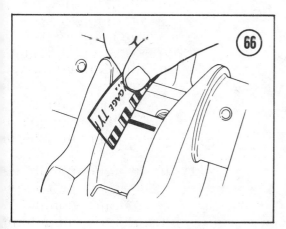

is acceptable. If the clearance is out of tolerance, have the crankshaft ground and proper bearings fitted.

OIL PUMP

Because of the difficulty in removing the oil sump from the engine while installed in car, be certain to service oil pump whenever the engine is removed. **Figure 67** is an exploded view of the oil pump.

Oil Pump Servicing

1. Remove the engine from the car as described in this chapter under *Engine Removal/Replacement*, or remove oil sump as described under *Oil Sump Removal/Installation*.

2. See **Figure 68**. Remove bolts holding the sprocket to oil pump, retaining plate to main bearing cap, and oil pump to crankcase.

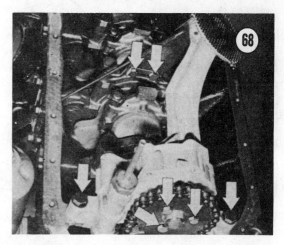

3. Remove oil pump from crankcase, as shown in **Figure 69**. Remove O-ring from housing and pressure relief pipe. If there are shims between the oil pump housing and the crankcase, note their position and mark them for later replacement. See **Figure 70**.

4. See **Figure 71**. Unscrew union (1) and remove compression spring (2) and plunger (3). Clean all parts thoroughly with a suitable solvent.

5. Remove bolts holding pump cover to pump body and remove cover.

6. Use a puller, as shown in **Figure 72**, to remove the drive flange from inner rotor. Before

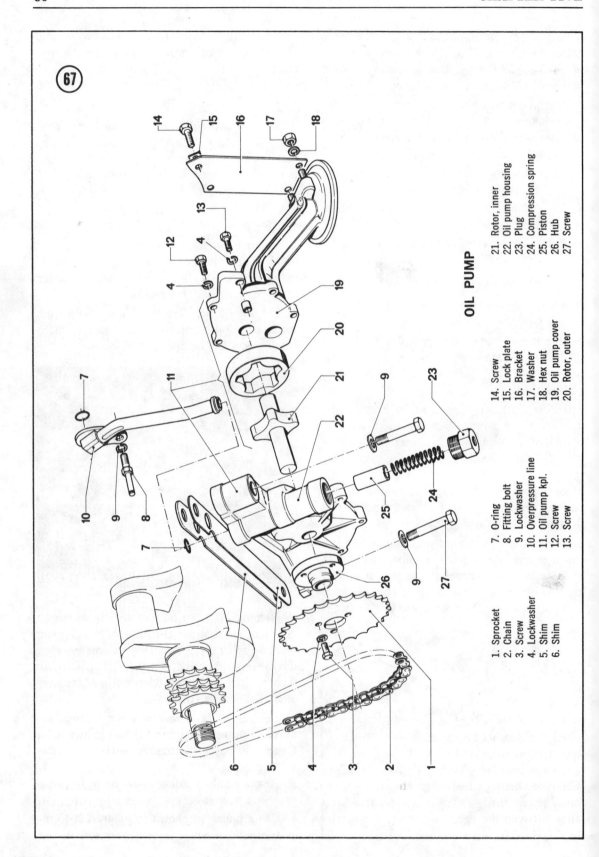

OIL PUMP

1. Sprocket
2. Chain
3. Screw
4. Lockwasher
5. Shim
6. Shim
7. O-ring
8. Fitting bolt
9. Lockwasher
10. Overpressure line
11. Oil pump kpl.
12. Screw
13. Screw
14. Screw
15. Lock plate
16. Bracket
17. Washer
18. Hex nut
19. Oil pump cover
20. Rotor, outer
21. Rotor, inner
22. Oil pump housing
23. Plug
24. Compression spring
25. Piston
26. Hub
27. Screw

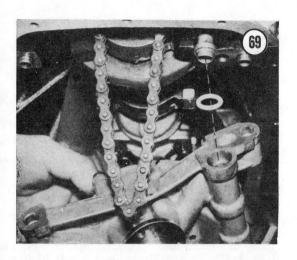

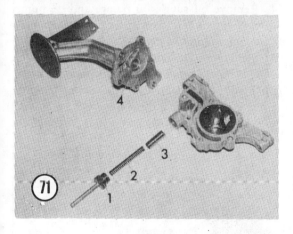

removal of the flange, use a feeler gauge to check the clearance between the outer rotor and the pump housing and between the inner rotor and outer rotor, as shown in **Figures 73 and 74**. Clearance between the outer rotor and housing must be less than 0.0059 in. (0.15mm). Clearance between the inner and outer rotor must be 0.0047-0.0118 in. (0.12-0.30mm).

7. If clearances are excessive, remove drive flange and replace defective parts.

8. Place a straightedge across the face of the housing and use a feeler gauge to measure the clearance between the rotors and pump housing face. Clearance should be 0.0014-0.0043 in. (0.036-0.109mm).

9. Check the free length of the compression spring. The spring should be 2.68 in. (68mm) long. If defective, replace.

10. Inspect all parts carefully for wear and damage. Check that the filter screen and oil passages are not clogged. Renew damaged parts as required.

11. Check that the inner rotor is attached firmly to drive flange without looseness or wobble. Replace defective parts.

12. To reassemble and install, reverse procedures used in dismantling and disassembly. See Figure 70. Adjust chain tension with compensating shims under oil pump body. Make certain oil passage is not blocked with shim. Always renew O-ring between housing and pressure relief pipe.

> NOTE: *The chain tension is correct when it can be depressed with light thumb pressure.*

13. When fitting the retaining plate to the oil pump, align and tighten the bolts so that the oil pump is in a tension free position.

Oil Pump Drive Chain
Removal/Installation

When servicing the oil pump, inspect the condition of the drive chain for wear and damage. Repair is by replacement.

1. Remove oil sump, as previously described.

2. Remove the timing chain as described in Chapter Six.

3. Remove bolts holding drive sprocket to drive flange. Remove sprocket as shown in **Figure 75**.

4. Remove chain from crankshaft sprocket and replace with new one. Replace sprocket with chain threaded around it. Replace bolts and tighten. Check chain tension as described above. If tension is not correct, insert or remove shims from under oil pump housing.

CRANKSHAFT/FLYWHEEL SERVICING

Servicing of the crankshaft requires removal of the engine from the car. Servicing of the flywheel can be performed with the engine removed or installed as long as the transmission, pressure plate, and clutch disc have been removed. **Figure 76** shows the detail of the crankshaft; **Figure 77** the flywheel.

Removal/Servicing

1. Remove the engine as described earlier in this chapter. Mount the engine on a stand or suitable workbench.

2. Remove the transmission, pressure plate, and clutch disc from the flywheel, as described in Chapter Ten.

3. Remove the timing chain, as previously described.

4. Remove oil sump, oil pump, and oil pump drive chain, as described in *Oil Sump Removal/ Installation* and *Oil Pump* above.

5. See **Figure 78**. With a dial gauge, check the end play of the crankshaft by moving it back and forth with a screwdriver at the center bearing. End play should be 0.0034 to 0.0069 in. (0.085 to 0.174mm). Excessive end play is corrected by

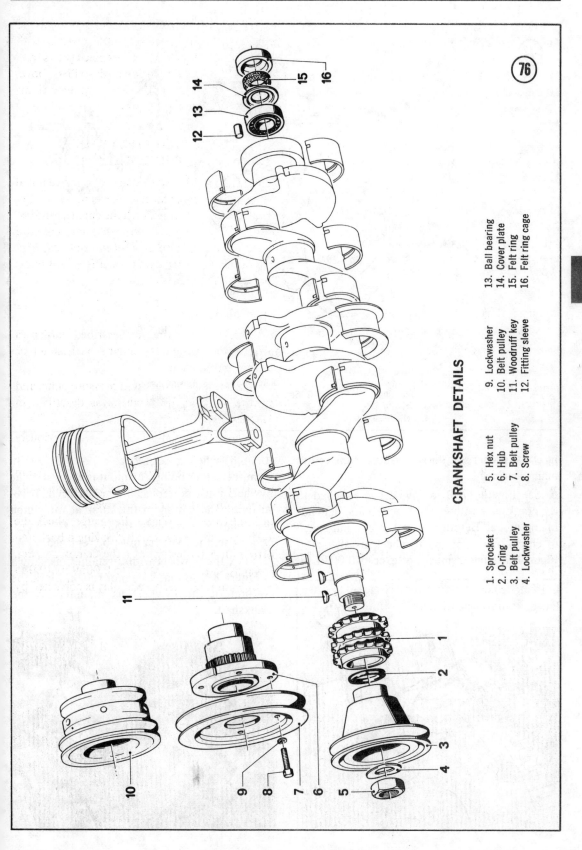

CRANKSHAFT DETAILS

1. Sprocket
2. O-ring
3. Belt pulley
4. Lockwasher
5. Hex nut
6. Hub
7. Belt pulley
8. Screw
9. Lockwasher
10. Belt pulley
11. Woodruff key
12. Fitting sleeve
13. Ball bearing
14. Cover plate
15. Felt ring
16. Felt ring cage

5

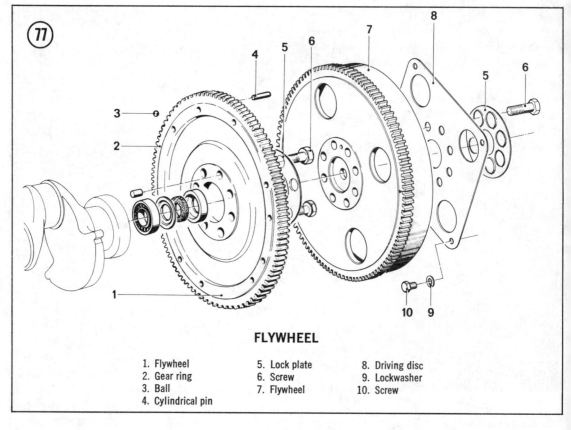

FLYWHEEL

1. Flywheel
2. Gear ring
3. Ball
4. Cylindrical pin

5. Lock plate
6. Screw
7. Flywheel

8. Driving disc
9. Lockwasher
10. Screw

inserting proper size thrust washers at the center main bearing.

6. See Figure 77. The flywheel is attached to the crankshaft with either 6 or 8 bolts, depending on model. Before removal, use a dial gauge to check runout of the flywheel, as shown in **Figure 79**. Runout must not exceed 0.0039 in.

(0.1mm) when measured at a point 7.874 in. from the center point. If runout is excessive, the flywheel must be replaced or resurfaced. If resurfaced, the minimum thickness at the clutch disc mating surface is 0.535 in. (13.6mm). Otherwise, the flywheel must be replaced.

7. Lock the flywheel with a retainer, as shown in **Figure 80**, so that it cannot rotate. Mark the position of the flywheel as mounted to the crankshaft.

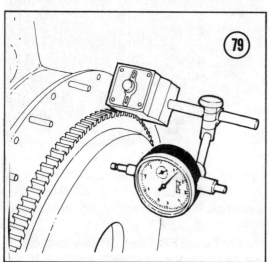

7007

8. *(8 bolts)* Unscrew and remove expansion bolts. Remove the flywheel from the crankshaft. During replacement, use new bolts and lock in place with a suitable locking compound, such as Loctite No. 41.

9. *(6 bolts)* Use a screwdriver to pry off the retaining plate, as shown in **Figure 81**. Unscrew the bolts and remove the flywheel. During installation, a new retaining plate must be used.

10. On models with a torque converter, unscrew the expansion bolts and renew the driving disc shown in **Figure 82**. Remove the flywheel from the crankshaft.

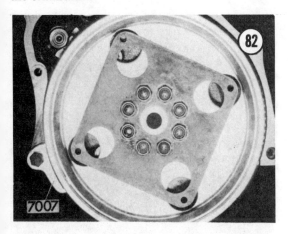

11. See **Figure 83**. Unscrew the bolts holding the rear cover to the cylinder block. Remove and discard gaskets. Inspect condition of the radial sealing ring mounted in the end cover. If it is damaged or shows signs of leaking, press it out and replace with new one.

12. Inspect flywheel and ring gear for signs of wear or damage. Check the ring gear for broken or missing teeth. If the flywheel is lightly scored, the damage may be milled off in a lathe. Deep scoring requires flywheel replacement.

13. If the ring gear is damaged and must be replaced, drill a hole with a 6mm drill in the ring gear, as shown in **Figure 84**. Be careful not to drill into flywheel. Use a chisel, as shown in **Figure 85**, to split the ring gear and remove it from the flywheel. To replace, heat the new starter ring gear to 450°F and install it to the flywheel with the aid of a brass punch, as shown in **Figure 86**. Make certain the tooth chamfer faces toward the crankshaft side.

14. Unscrew nut holding belt pulley to crankshaft. Remove nut, lockwasher, and pulley from crankshaft. Remove Woodruff key from crankshaft.

15. See **Figure 87**. Check the condition of the gear teeth on the crankshaft sprocket. If the

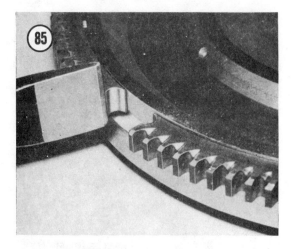

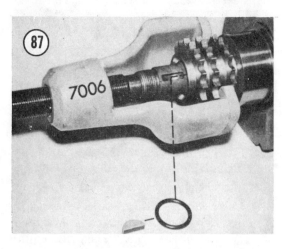

16. Rotate crankshaft until No. 1 piston is at TDC. See **Figure 88**. Remove nuts holding connecting rod and end cap to connecting rod. Remove end cap and rod bearing. Gently push connecting rod up into cylinder until the crankshaft can be rotated without hitting the connecting rod. Repeat this procedure for the other connecting rods.

17. See **Figure 89**. Remove the bolts holding the 5 main bearing caps to the block and crankshaft. Remove the main bearing caps and bearings from crankshaft. Note that the center bearing cap also holds the oil pump retainer.

sprocket is damaged or if the O-ring has been leaking, remove the Woodruff key, O-ring, and use a puller to remove the sprocket. Always replace the O-ring with a new one whenever the crankshaft pulley is removed.

18. Lift out the crankshaft and remove upper part of main bearings from cylinder block.

19. Check the main bearings and connecting rod bearings for signs of scoring, wear, and seizing. If the bearings appear satisfactory,

check clearance between them and the journals, as previously described under *Connecting Rod Bearings*. Clearance should be 0.0019-0.0027 in. (0.030-0.070mm). If the clearance is excessive, have the crankshaft reground and fitted with proper size bearings.

> NOTE: *The crankshaft is marked with either red or blue marks that indicate the original grind of the crankshaft. Main bearings must be used that are of the same color markings. Reground crankshafts are marked, as shown in* **Figure 90**. *The connecting rod and main bearings must have the same color coding.*

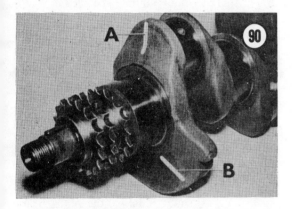

20. Use a micrometer to measure crankshaft pins and journal. Measure diameter at various points to determine wear, taper, and out-of-round conditions.

21. Check the dimensions against specifications. If the measurements indicate excessive wear, have the crankshaft reground to suit the nearest undersize bearings. Refer such service to your BMW dealer.

22. Check crankshaft for bends at the center journal. Support both ends of the crankshaft in a fixture so that it can be rotated. Mount a dial gauge so that it rides on the center journal. Rotate crankshaft and take readings. Maximum permissible bend is 0.0008 in. (0.02mm). Straighten or replace crankshaft, as required.

23. Use an extractor to remove the ball bearing (1), cover plate (2), felt ring (3), and felt ring cage from rear end of crankshaft. See **Figure 91**. Inspect parts for wear or damage. Replace as required. To install, pack the ball

bearing with multipurpose grease, fit cover plate with imprint facing outwards, impregnate the felt ring in hot tallow, and tap the felt ring cage into place until it seats securely.

MANIFOLD SERVICING

Whenever the engine is disassembled or service is required to the cylinder head, valves, or pistons, the intake and exhaust manifolds must be removed and gaskets replaced during installation. To remove the manifolds, locate and remove the nuts and washers holding the manifolds to the engine. Inspect carefully for cracks or defects and replace as required.

ENGINE REASSEMBLY

Engine reassembly is the reverse of procedures used during disassembly. The following steps detail required actions and checks. Make certain the assembly area is clean and that all needed parts and supplies are available before starting work. Lubricate all bearing, bushing, and journal mating surfaces liberally before assembly.

1. Place the crankcase upside down on a holding fixture or work bench.

2. Fit the upper half of the main bearings to their seats in the crankcase. Make certain the locating tabs insert into the seats.

3. Lower the crankshaft carefully into place on top of the main bearings.

4. Insert lower half of main bearings into bearing caps and fit the main bearing caps to the crankshaft. Install cap bolts to caps and torque tighten to 44 ft.-lb.

5. Check crankshaft end play, as previously described. If excessive, correct with proper size center main bearing and thrust washers.

5

6. Fit the gasket and the rear crankcase cover plate to the crankcase. Insert and tighten mounting bolts.

7. Install the flywheel to the crankshaft with the special bolts and washers. Install the retaining plate (if so equipped). Torque tighten bolts to 85 ft.-lb.

8. Assemble connecting rod and piston assembly, as previously described. Insert connecting rod assemblies into cylinders. Be careful that connecting rods do not damage crankshaft journals.

9. Fit connecting rods, bearings, and caps to crankshaft. Torque tighten bolts to 40 ft.-lb.

10. Install crankshaft sprocket to crankshaft.

11. Install oil pump. Connect oil pump drive chain to crankshaft sprocket.

12. Install oil sump to bottom of block. Make certain to coat mating surface of rear cover and oil sump with gasket compound. Torque tighten fixing bolts to 57 ft.-lb.

13. Install the camshaft and valve assemblies to the cylinder head. Rotate the crankshaft until No. 1 piston is at top dead center on the compression stroke.

14. Install camshaft in head so that the camshaft sprocket mounting plate is positioned as shown in Figure 27. The notch in the flange must be in alignment with cast nose in cylinder head. The bore for the set pin faces downward. Loosen adjustment nut on rocker arms.

15. Place the cylinder head gasket on the block. Make certain the water and oil passage holes are in alignment. Gently lower the cylinder head onto the head gasket.

16. Insert head bolts with washers through head into block. See Figure 28, which shows the cylinder head bolt tightening sequence. Sequentially tighten each bolt to 30 ft.-lb. Then sequentially tighten each bolt to 45 ft.-lb., and finally to about 55 ft.-lb.

17. Install the camshaft drive sprocket to the camshaft sprocket mounting plate.

18. Install chain tensioner rail and guide rail to block. Install chain around camshaft driven sprocket and crankshaft drive sprocket. Install and bleed chain tensioner piston, as previously described.

19. Make certain the camshaft is still properly aligned and that the chain has been installed correctly according to marks previously made.

20. Adjust the valve clearance, as previously described.

21. Install gaskets and mount upper and lower timing gear covers to cylinder block and head. Install bolts and tighten securely. Make certain to coat the mating surfaces between the upper and lower cover, and the lower cover and sump thoroughly with gasket compound. Install and tighten nuts fixing upper cover to lower cover.

22. Install crankshaft pulley to crankshaft. Torque tighten fixing bolt to 100 ft.-lb.

23. Install the water pump as specified in Chapter Eight.

24. Fit alternator mounting bracket to cylinder block and mount alternator to bracket with fixing bolts. Install and adjust belt to water pump and alternator and belt to air pump. On 2002ti, install drive belt to air injection unit.

25. Install fuel pump assembly to cylinder head.

26. Install the oil filter.

27. Install intake and exhaust manifolds with associated gaskets.

28. Install all other parts that were removed. These would include the carburetor(s), air pump, fuel injection system (if so equipped), cylinder head cover, distributor, spark plugs, and wiring. The alignment marks on the distributor and crankshaft pulley should be aligned, as shown in Figure 24.

29. If the engine has not been removed, make certain to connect all wires and hoses. Make certain to add engine oil and coolant before starting the engine.

ENGINE INSTALLATION

Check the engine carefully to make certain that all parts and assemblies have been installed. Reverse the procedures used during removal to install the engine and transmission. When installed in the car, make certain to connect all wires and hoses, fill the engine to the proper level with oil, and fill the radiator with coolant.

After starting, check carefully for oil and coolant leaks. Check and adjust engine timing as required.

$D = 5.25$

$\pi D = 16.4934$"

$25° = 1.145$" $\frac{9}{64} = .140625$

$20° = .9162$ $\frac{29}{32} = .90625$

$\frac{59}{64} = .921875$

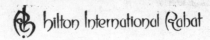

Où êtes Vous ?
Where are you?

En indiquant le lieu où vous vous trouvez il nous sera très facile de vous appeler. Merci.

Expecting a phone call or a visitor?
By filling in this form we will know where to locate you. Thank you

Nom / Name ....
Chambre / Room N° ....

Priere de remettre cet imprimé au concierge
Please hand this over to the concierge

O   Al foroussia Coffee Shop
O   Chellah Grill
O   Echrob ou Chouf bar
O   Bab Es Sama Restaurant Marocain
O   Piscine/Swiming Pool
O   Sauna

O   ————————————————

Date ————————— Heure —————————

Table 1   SPECIFICATIONS, TOLERANCES, AND TORQUE TIGHTENING

Description	Specification
Compression Test	
Good	above 149.3 psi
Normal	135.1 to 149.3 psi
Poor	below 128 psi
Oil Pump Chain Length	44 links
Valve Clearances	
(Operating Temperature)	0.0079-0.0098 in. (0.20-0.25mm)
(Cold)	0.0059-0.0079 in. (0.15-0.20mm)

Sequence of Valve Adjustment	TDC on No.	Valve Overlap on No.
	1	4
	3	2
	4	1
	2	3

Description	Specification
Valve Timing	
Intake Opens	4° BTDC
Intake Closes	52° ABDC
Exhaust Opens	52° BBDC
Exhaust Closes	4° ATDC
Total Period	236°
Valves	
Overall Length Intake	4.087 ± 0.00079 in. (103.8 ± 0.2mm)
Overall Length Exhaust	4.106 ± 0.00079 in. (104.3 ± 0.2mm)
Valve Head Diameter Intake	1.732 in. (44mm), 1.654 in. (42mm) 1600 model
Valve Head Diameter Exhaust	1.496 in. (38mm), 1.378 in. (35mm) 1600 model
Valve Stem Diameter Intake	0.315 in. (8mm)
Valve Stem Diameter Exhaust	0.315 in. (8mm)
New Valve Edge Thickness Intake	0.059 ± 0.0004 in. (1.5 ± 0.1mm)
New Valve Edge Thickness Exhaust	0.08 ± 0.0004 in. (2.0 ± 0.1mm)
Minimum Edge Thickness Intake	0.039 ± 0.0004 in. (1.0 ± 0.1mm)
Minimum Edge Thickness Exhaust	0.059 ± 0.0004 in. (1.5 ± 0.1mm)
Valve Seat Angle Intake	45° 20'
Valve Seat Angle Exhaust	45° 20'
Valve Shrink Fit in Head	0.00394-0.00591 in. (0.10-0.15mm)
Valve Seat Angle	45°
Outer Correction Angle	15°
Valve Seat Width Intake	0.063-0.079 in. (1.6-2.0mm)
Valve Seat Width Exhaust	0.079-0.095 in. (2.0-2.4mm)
Valve Guides	
Overall Length	2.047 in. (52mm)
Outer Diameter	0.5512 in. (14mm)
Inner Diameter	0.3150 in. (8mm)
Shrink Fit in Cylinder Head	0.0013-0.0027 in. (0.033-0.069mm)
Valve Running Clearances	
Intake	0.00098-0.00216 in. (0.025-0.055mm)
Exhaust	0.00157-0.00275 in. (0.040-0.070mm)

(continued)

5

Table 1   SPECIFICATIONS, TOLERANCES, AND TORQUE TIGHTENING   (continued)

Description	Specification
Valve Springs	
Free Length of Spring	1.7126 in. (43.5mm)
Camshaft	
Diameters	1.3780-1.6536-1.6929 in. (35-42-43mm)
	−0.0006 in. (0.016mm)
Cylinder Head Bores	1.3780-1.6536-1.6929 in. (35-42-43mm)
	+0.001 in. (+0.025mm)
Clearance	0.00134-0.00295 in. (0.034-0.075mm)
Axial Play	0.00079-0.00512 in. (0.02-0.13mm)
Chain Tensioner	
Piston Length	2.441 in. (62mm)
Compression Spring Free Length	6.122 in. (155.5mm)
Crankshaft	
Diameter of Bearing Bore	
Red	2.362 in. (60mm)
Blue	2.362 in. (60mm)
Bearing Shell Thickness	
Red	0.0984 in. (2.50mm)
Blue	0.0988 in. (2.51mm)
Main Bearing Journal Diameter	
Red	2.165 in. (55mm)
Blue	2.165 in. (55mm)
Radial Bearing Play	
Red	0.00118-0.002756 in. (0.030-0.070mm)
Blue	0.00118-0.002677 in. (0.030-0.068mm)
Connecting Rod Journal Diameter	1.8898 in. (48mm)
Crankshaft Endplay	0.00335-0.00685 in. (0.085-0.174mm)
Center Main Bearing Runout	0.0008 in. (0.02mm)
Connecting Rods	
Overall Length	5.315 in. (135mm)
Small End Bushing Inner Diameter	0.866 in. (22mm)
Bearing Shell Thickness	0.0781-0.0785 in. (1.983-1.993mm)
Radial Bearing Play	0.00090-0.00272 in. (0.023-0.069mm)
Permitted Weight Difference	0.142 oz.
Cylinders	
Maximum Out-of-Round	0.00039 in. (0.01mm)
Maximum Bore Taper	0.00039 in. (0.01mm)
Maximum Wear on Piston and Cylinder	0.0039-0.0059 in. (0.10-0.15mm)
Piston	
Weight Group	+ or−, stamped
Piston Pin Class	W or S, stamped
Piston Pin Diameter	
A	3.3055 in. (83.96mm)
B	3.3059 in. (83.97mm)
C	3.3063 in. (83.98mm)
Piston Installed Clearance	0.00157 in. (0.040mm)
Permitted Weight Difference	0.32-0.35 oz.

(continued)

Table 1   SPECIFICATIONS, TOLERANCES, AND TORQUE TIGHTENING   (continued)

Description	Specification
Piston Rings	
1st Groove Height	0.0689 in. (1.75mm)
1st Ring End Gap	0.0118-0.0177 in. (0.3-0.45mm)
1st Ring Flank Clearance	0.00059-0.00114 in. (0.015-0.029mm)
2nd Groove Height	0.0787 in. (2mm)
2nd Ring End Gap	0.0118-0.0177 in. (0.3-0.45mm)
2nd Ring Flank Clearance	0.00047-0.00102 in. (0.012-0.026mm)
3rd Groove Height	0.1575 in. (4mm)
3rd Ring End Gap	0.0098-0.0157 in. (0.25-0.40mm)
3rd Ring Flank Clearance	0.00043-0.00098 in. (0.011-0.025mm)
Piston Pins	
Offset from Piston Centerline	0.0591 in. (1.5mm)
Inside Diameter	
W Stamped on Piston Crown	0.86626-0.86640 in. (22.003-22.005mm)
S Stamped on Piston Crown	0.86618-0.86626 in. (22.001-22.003mm)
Clearance in Piston	0.0004-0.00020 in. (0.001-0.005mm)
Connecting Rod Bushing Play	
White	0.00012-0.00039 in. (0.003-0.010mm)
Black	0.00020-0.00047 in. (0.005-0.012mm)
Flywheel	
Maximum Imbalance	5 cmp
Maximum Runout	0.00394 in. (0.1mm)
Minimum Thickness at Friction Surface	0.5354 in. (13.6mm)
Maximum Machining of Friction Surface	0.0157 in. (0.4mm)
Tightening Torque (ft.-lb.)	
Cylinder Head Bolts	
1st Stage	30
2nd Stage	45
3rd Stage	55
Main Bearing Caps	42-45.6
Connecting Rod Bolts	37.6-41.2
Flywheel to Crankshaft	83.4-90.6
Chain Tensioner Bolt	21.7-28.9
Rocker Set Screw	6.5-7.9
Oil Pump Relief Valve Plug	18.1-21.7
Oil Supply Bolt to Camshaft	8.0-10.1
Crankshaft Pulley	101.3
Spark Plugs	18.1-21.7
Fuel Pump	8.6
Carburetor to Manifold	7.2-10.1
Timing Case Cover Top to Bottom	6.5
Distributor Flange	18.1
Filter to Upper Section	18.1

5

CHAPTER SIX

FUEL AND EXHAUST SYSTEMS

This chapter provides information on the fuel and exhaust systems. Included are the fuel tank, fuel lines, fuel pump, carburetor, intake/exhaust manifolds, mufflers, exhaust pipes, and air cleaner.

Fuel is pumped from the fuel tank through the fuel lines by the fuel pump, which is either mechanically or electrically operated, depending on car model. It is then fed to the carburetor(s) or fuel injection device where it is mixed with air and fed to the combustion chambers through the intake manifold. After combustion, exhaust gases are expelled from the combustion chambers through the exhaust manifold to the exhaust pipes and muffler, and ultimately out through the tailpipes.

WARNING
Extreme care should be used when servicing the various parts of the fuel system to minimize the danger of fire or explosion. Before servicing fuel tank or lines, make certain that fuel is completely drained into a suitable sealed container. Residual gases in the tank should be expelled by filling the tank completely with an inert gas or, as a last resort, water. Soldering or welding the tank should be done with it full of inert gas or water. If water is used, be certain to dry the inside of the tank thoroughly before refilling with fuel.

FUEL TANK

Removal/Installation

1. Disconnect battery ground strap.
2. Remove drain plug and drain fuel into suitable container.
3. Open the trunk and remove the floor panel, which exposes the fuel tank.
4. See **Figure 1**. Disconnect positive lead (1) from socket (2) on immersion tube transmitter. Detach ground lead (3).

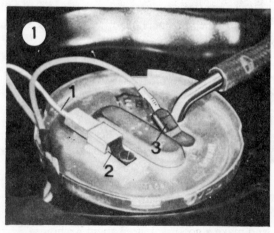

5. Pull off fuel hose from immersion tube transmitter.

6. See **Figure 2**. Detach hose clamp at bottom of filler neck and push rubber sleeve upwards.

7. Unscrew fuel tank securing bolts and lift out the fuel tank upwards. See **Figure 3**.

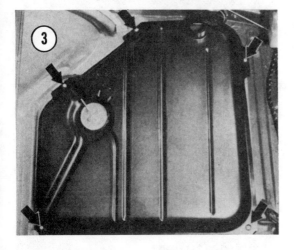

8. Use 2 crossed screwdrivers, as shown in **Figure 4**, to unscrew the immersion tube transmitter in a counterclockwise direction.

9. Inspect the fuel tank for damage or leaks. If defective, weld, solder, or renew, as appropriate.

10. Check the condition of the immersion tube transmitter and clean the fine mesh screen with clean fuel. See **Figure 5**. Check the condition of the radial cord seal (1) for damage. Replace as required. When refitting the seal, coat it with Vaseline. It will swell upon contact with fuel and make a good seal after about 48 hours.

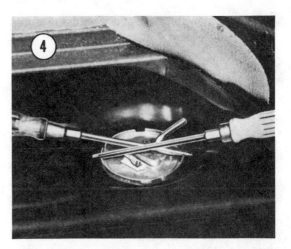

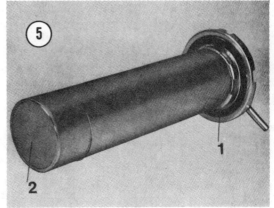

FUEL LINES

The fuel line is connected at one end to the fuel tank and at the other end to the intake side of the fuel pump. Another line leads from the outlet side of the fuel pump to the carburetor. Periodically inspect the fuel lines for damage and leaks. Pay special attention to the condition of the rubber sections, as they deteriorate with time. Replace as required.

FUEL PUMP

On most models, the fuel pump is located on the left side of the cylinder head and is mechanically driven through a connecting rod that rubs on a lobe of the camshaft. In the 2002tii, the fuel pump is electrically operated and starts to operate when the ignition key is switched on even though the engine may not be running.

Fine mesh filters are incorporated into the pumps to prevent foreign material from entering the carburetion system.

Figure 6 (next page) is an exploded diagram of the mechanically operated fuel pump.

Filter Cleaning

The filter can be cleaned with the fuel pump mounted to the engine.

1. (*1600*) See **Figure 7**. Remove bolt from center of cover. Remove cover and seal and lift out the strainer. Be careful not to let any foreign material enter the fuel pump. Clean the strainer with clean fuel and inspect for damage and rust. If defective, replace strainer. Inspect and replace seal if damaged.

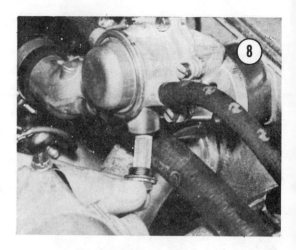

2. (*2002, 2002A, 2002ti*) See **Figure 8**. Unscrew and remove bolt, seal, and strainer. Clean the strainer with clean fuel and inspect for damage or rust. If defective, replace. Inspect and replace seal if damaged.

Pressure Testing

1. See **Figure 9**. Attach a pressure tester to the fuel pump and carburetor, as shown.

2. Start the engine and read pressure on the gauge. If the pressure is less than 0.7 psi, the pump is defective and should be serviced or replaced.

3. At the carburetor, press down the float needle valve. The pressure should be 4.1 to 4.3 psi and must remain constant. If pressure falls, replace the float needle valve in the carburetor.

4. (*2002ti*) Set up the test equipment as shown in **Figure 10**. Press down each float needle valve individually and read the meter. Pressures should be as given above. If not, replace defective float needle valve.

Disassembly/Servicing

1. Remove hoses attached to fuel pump.

2. See Figure 6. Remove bolts fixing fuel pump to insulating flange and cylinder head. Remove fuel pump and insulating flange.

3. Withdraw pump plunger and inspect for wear and damage. If defective, replace.

4. Inspect condition of insulating flange. Replace if defective.

5. Mark the top and bottom halves of the fuel pump body. See **Figure 11**. Unscrew bolt (1), remove washer (2) and cover (3), and withdraw

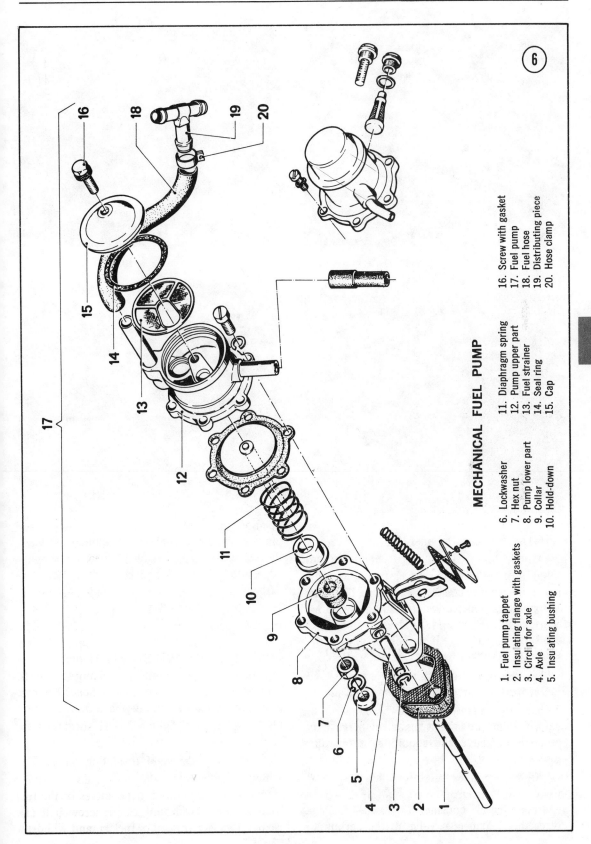

MECHANICAL FUEL PUMP

1. Fuel pump tappet
2. Insulating flange with gaskets
3. Circl p for axle
4. Axle
5. Insulating bushing
6. Lockwasher
7. Hex nut
8. Pump lower part
9. Collar
10. Hold-down
11. Diaphragm spring
12. Pump upper part
13. Fuel strainer
14. Seal ring
15. Cap
16. Screw with gasket
17. Fuel pump
18. Fuel hose
19. Distributing piece
20. Hose clamp

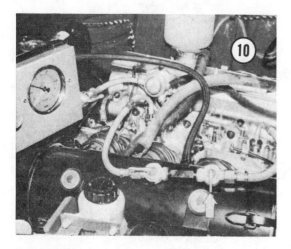

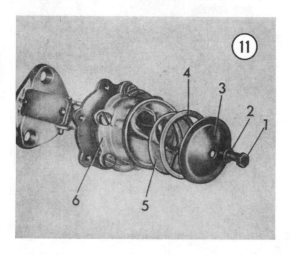

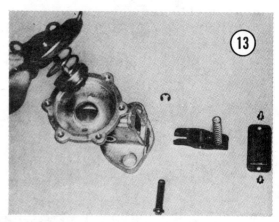

seal (4) and fine mesh strainer (5). Loosen screws and remove top of pump (6) from diaphragm and lower half of pump.

6. (*2002, 2002A, 2002ti*) See **Figure 12**. Mark the top and bottom halves of the pump; remove the top half. Loosen intake valve (1) and check seal surface. Replace if defective. Check the output valve (2) for ease of operation. Replace if defective.

7. Dismantle the bottom half of the fuel pump, as shown in **Figure 13**.

8. Inspect all parts for wear and damage. Pay special attention to the condition of the diaphragm. It must not show any signs of cracks or hardening. Replace defective parts with new ones.

9. To reassemble and install, reverse the steps given above. During reassembly, be certain to position the diaphragm correctly. Always replace gaskets and seals with new ones. Check the fuel pump mating surface with a straightedge, and if distorted, replace.

10. To test operation of the fuel pump before installation, connect a 3 foot piece of fuel line or hose between the intake to the fuel pump and the fuel line from the fuel tank. Hold the fuel pump considerably above its normal mounting location. Operate the plunger by hand. If fuel is drawn up to the pump soon after the pumping action is started, the pump is satisfactory.

CARBURETORS

Several different models and types of carburetors have been used depending on model. This section provides information on all of the carburetors except for the fuel injection system used on the 2002tii. Service to the fuel injection system should be referred to a BMW dealer due to the need of special equipment and knowledge.

Figure 14 is an exploded view of the single, dual throat, downdraft carburetor used on the 1600 and early 2002 models. **Figure 15** shows the detail of the early 2002A carburetor. **Figure 16** shows the Solex 32/32 DIDTA carburetor used on later 2002 models. **Figures 17 and 18** are exploded views of the dual sidedraft carburetor used on the 2002ti.

A carburetor in good operating condition will deliver the proper gasoline and air ratios for all engine running speeds. A gradual decline in smoothness, response, and power will occur as the carburetor slips from adjustment and its delicate parts become dirty and worn.

Accurate calibration of passages and discharge holes require that extreme care be taken in disassembly, cleaning and reassembly. Use only a high-grade carburetor cleaner and compressed air to clean parts and passages. Never use wire or other pointed instruments for cleaning; calibration of the carburetor will be affected. See Chapter Four, *Engine Tune-Up*, for engine idle speed adjustment procedures.

Fuel Level Adjusting

1. Warm up the engine and remove fuel intake hose from carburetor.

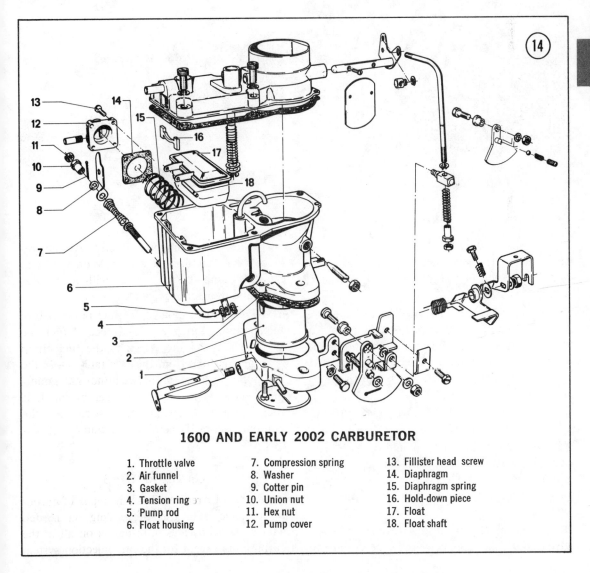

1600 AND EARLY 2002 CARBURETOR

1. Throttle valve	7. Compression spring	13. Fillister head screw
2. Air funnel	8. Washer	14. Diaphragm
3. Gasket	9. Cotter pin	15. Diaphragm spring
4. Tension ring	10. Union nut	16. Hold-down piece
5. Pump rod	11. Hex nut	17. Float
6. Float housing	12. Pump cover	18. Float shaft

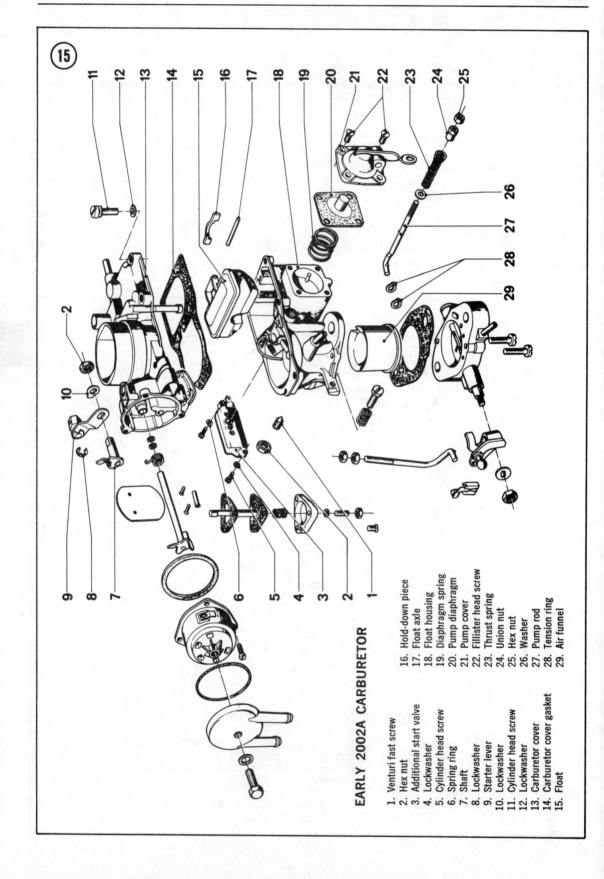

⑮

EARLY 2002A CARBURETOR

1. Venturi fast screw
2. Hex nut
3. Additional start valve
4. Lockwasher
5. Cylinder head screw
6. Spring ring
7. Shaft
8. Lockwasher
9. Starter lever
10. Lockwasher
11. Cylinder head screw
12. Lockwasher
13. Carburetor cover
14. Carburetor cover gasket
15. Float
16. Hold-down piece
17. Float axle
18. Float housing
19. Diaphragm spring
20. Pump diaphragm
21. Pump cover
22. Fillister head screw
23. Thrust spring
24. Union nut
25. Hex nut
26. Washer
27. Pump rod
28. Tension ring
29. Air funnel

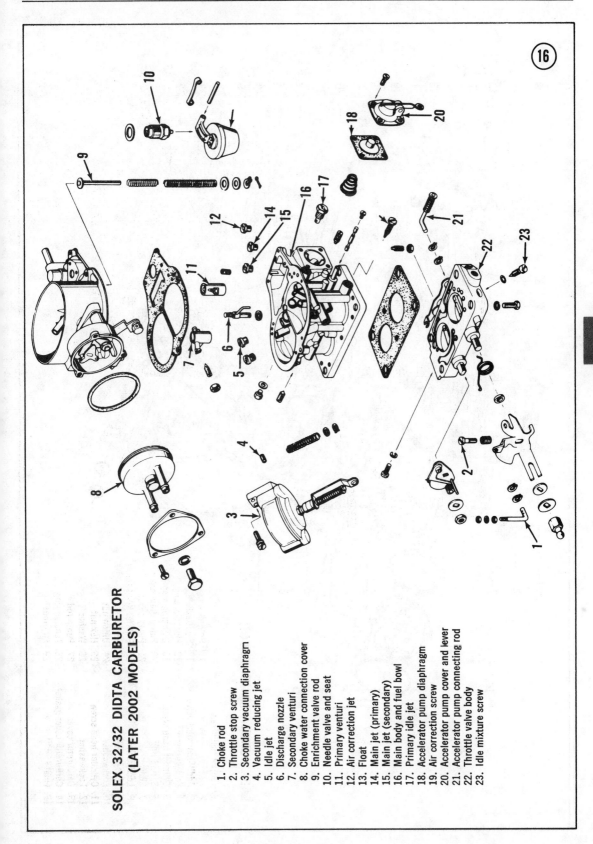

SOLEX 32/32 DIDTA CARBURETOR (LATER 2002 MODELS)

1. Choke rod
2. Throttle stop screw
3. Secondary vacuum diaphragm
4. Vacuum reducing jet
5. Idle jet
6. Discharge nozzle
7. Secondary venturi
8. Choke water connection cover
9. Enrichment valve rod
10. Needle valve and seat
11. Primary venturi
12. Air correction jet
13. Float
14. Main jet (primary)
15. Main jet (secondary)
16. Main body and fuel bowl
17. Primary idle jet
18. Accelerator pump diaphragm
19. Air correction screw
20. Accelerator pump cover and lever
21. Accelerator pump connecting rod
22. Throttle valve body
23. Idle mixture screw

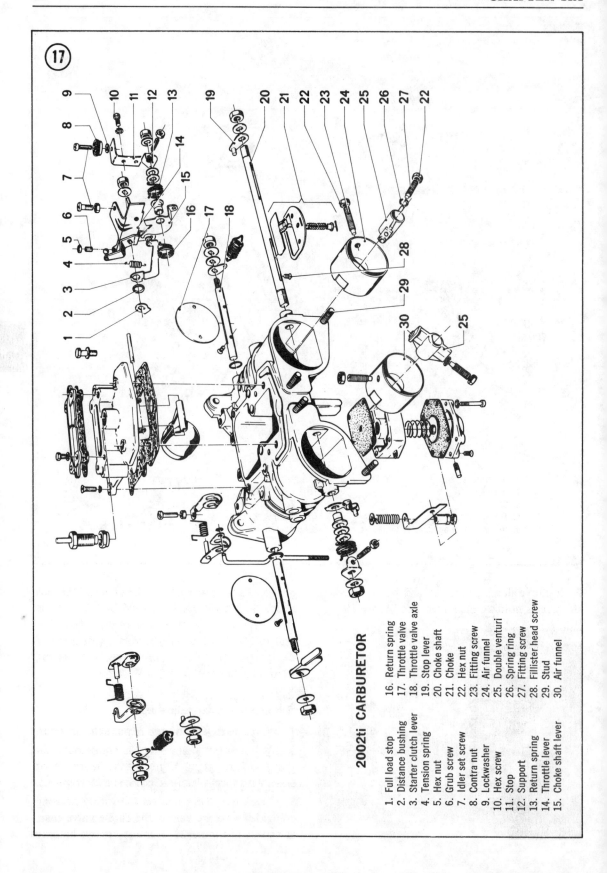

2002ti CARBURETOR

1. Full load stop
2. Distance bushing
3. Starter clutch lever
4. Tension spring
5. Hex nut
6. Grub screw
7. Idler set screw
8. Contra nut
9. Lockwasher
10. Hex screw
11. Stop
12. Support
13. Return spring
14. Throttle lever
15. Choke shaft lever
16. Return spring
17. Throttle valve
18. Throttle valve axle
19. Stop lever
20. Choke shaft
21. Choke
22. Hex nut
23. Fitting screw
24. Air funnel
25. Double venturi
26. Spring ring
27. Fitting screw
28. Fillister head screw
29. Stud
30. Air funnel

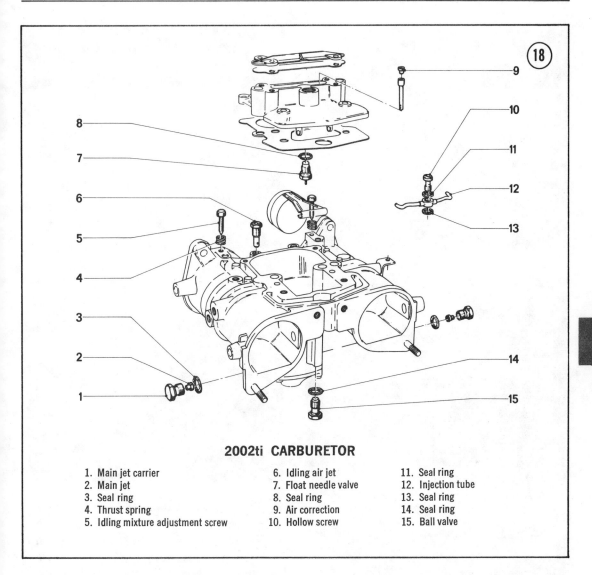

2002ti CARBURETOR

1. Main jet carrier
2. Main jet
3. Seal ring
4. Thrust spring
5. Idling mixture adjustment screw
6. Idling air jet
7. Float needle valve
8. Seal ring
9. Air correction
10. Hollow screw
11. Seal ring
12. Injection tube
13. Seal ring
14. Seal ring
15. Ball valve

2. Remove float cover and seal by unscrewing the screws holding the cover. See **Figure 19**.

3. Use a gauge to measure the depth of the fuel in the float bowl. Depth should be 0.7-0.75 in. (17-19mm). If level is incorrect, adjust the seal under the float needle valve. Checking of the level in the 2002ti requires special tools and should be referred to a BMW dealer.

Automatic Choke Adjusting

1. Warm up the engine and remove the air filter.

2. With a finger, make sure the choke butterfly shaft rotates easily. If necessary, lubricate or clean with spray cleaner. See **Figure 20** (typical).

3. Check that the notch on the spring housing coincides with the peg on the choke valve case, as shown in **Figure 21**. Remove screws holding

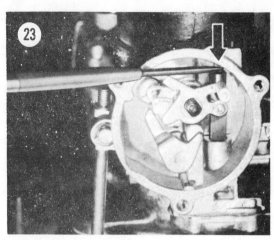

5. If opening is not correct, loosen nut (1) in **Figure 24** and adjust the butterfly valve.

spring housing to carburetor. Remove spring cover, as shown in **Figure 22**.

6. To install, check the heating element current. It should be approximately one amp at 12 volts. Check bimetallic spring for correct position in engaging piece, as shown in Figure 22. If either the electrical characteristics or bimetallic spring are defective, replace both with new units.

Fast Idle Speed Adjusting

1. Warm up the engine, hook up a tachometer, and set the fast idling speed to 2,100 rpm.

2. Move the accelerator rod until the choke butterfly can be closed by hand. See **Figure 25**. Close the butterfly valve to about 0.25 in. (6.5mm). This brings the stop lever to the fast idle speed. Do not move the accelerator rod again.

4. See **Figure 23**. Press choke rod down to the stop, as shown. Use a drill shank to measure the opening of the butterfly valve. The gap should be 0.259 in. (6.6mm).

3. See **Figure 26**. Use the adjusting nuts to increase or decrease the length of the rod. To reduce rpm, shorten the rod; to increase rpm, lengthen the rod.

Thermostat Valve Checking

See **Figure 27**. At 59°F valve (A) must be in the open position and be raised off the seat.

1. Remove thermostat valve cover.

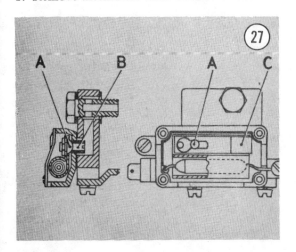

2. Switch on the ignition when the temperature is below 59°F. After about one minute, the bimetallic spring (C) must lift the valve 0.04-0.08 in. (1-2mm).

3. If the valve does not lift, the resistance is faulty or there is no current reaching the plug. If defective, do not try to repair. Replace with new unit.

Carburetor Removal/Installation

1. (*1600, 2002*) Remove the air filter and fuel hose leading to carburetor. See **Figure 28**. Loosen clamp screw (1) and clamp (2). Withdraw choke cable. To install choke cable, make certain that the (A) dimension of the sheath does not exceed 0.6 in. (15mm). Next, push the choke knob on the instrument into the bottom notch. Press the choke lever (3) against the stop and tighten the clamp screw.

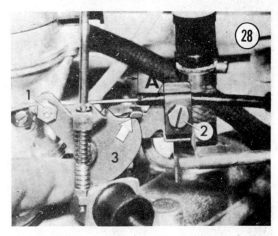

2. (*1600, 2002*) See **Figure 29**. Press off the clamp spring, detach the accelerator rod, draw off the vacuum hose, and loosen the nuts fixing the carburetor to the intake manifold. Lift up and remove the carburetor and gaskets. When installing, always replace the old gaskets with new ones.

3. (*2002A*) See **Figure 30**. Remove air cleaner and fuel line leading to carburetor. Remove cable from thermostat valve. Unscrew screws and remove choke mechanism cover. To install the cover, make certain the bimetallic spring is properly engaged in the cover and position the notch on the choke cover to coincide with the projection on the choke housing.

6

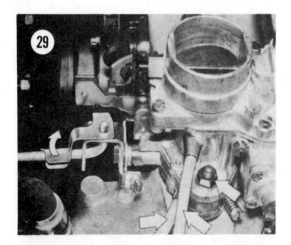

5. (*2002ti*) See **Figure 32**. Remove the air cleaner housing. Remove the choke cable from the bracket by loosening the fixing screw. During installation, make certain the cable sheath does not extend more than 0.6 in. (15mm) beyond the clamp. Place choke control on instrument panel into bottom notch and clamp the choke cable tightly. Finish removal by loosening the oil dipstick retainer and pulling off the fuel hoses.

6. (*2002ti*) See **Figure 33**. Remove the tension spring, loosen the bracket, and press the pull rod (1) away from the rotary shaft. Remove the nuts fixing the carburetor to the intake manifold. Remove the carburetor and gaskets. When installing, replace gaskets with new ones. During installation, insert the lug into the choke butterfly lever on the right hand carburetor before attaching the carburetor.

4. (*2002A*) See **Figure 31**. Remove the safety clip (1) and press rotary shaft downward. Pull off vacuum hoses. Loosen nuts holding carburetor to intake manifold. Remove carburetor and gaskets. When installing, replace the gaskets with new ones.

Float Servicing

1. *(1600, 2002)* Remove air cleaner housing and carburetor cover, as shown in **Figure 34**. When installing, always renew gasket. Remove clamp holding float and float pin in position. Remove float and pin. Inspect all parts for damage. The float should not have any cracks in the case or fuel inside. If it does, replace with new one.

2. *(2002A)* See **Figure 35**. Remove air cleaner housing and pull off cable from the thermostat valve. Remove fuel hose. Remove the clamp spring (2), draw out choke rod (3), remove screws from float cover, and remove float cover. Lift out the clamp holding float and float pin in position. Remove float and pin. Inspect all parts for damage. The float should not have any cracks in the case or fuel inside. If it does, replace with new one.

3. *(2002ti)* See **Figure 36**. Remove bolts fixing float cover and remove float cover. Press out the

float pin and remove the float. When installing, always replace gasket.

Float Needle Valve Servicing

1. *(1600, 2002)* Remove air cleaner housing and then the float cover. See **Figure 37** (typical). Unscrew float needle (1) and remove. During installation, always replace the gasket with a new one. The seal under the float needle can be varied in thickness to regulate the fuel level in the float bowl.

2. *(2002A)* Lift out spring clamp and remove choke rod. Pull off fuel hose and cable from the thermostat valve. Remove float cover, screw out float needle valve and seal, and remove gasket. During installation always replace the gasket with a new one. The seal under the float needle can be varied in thickness to regulate the fuel level in the float bowl.

3. *(2002ti)* Remove the float bowl cover and gasket. Unscrew the float needle valve from the

center of the float cover. The thickness of the seal under the float needle valve can alter the fuel level.

Carburetor Cleaning

The carburetor should be dismantled at least every 24,000 miles and cleaned thoroughly. Overhaul kits are available, and include gaskets, seals, needle valves, and other parts subject to wear or deterioration.

When dismantling, make certain to identify all parts for later replacement. Soak parts in a good quality carburetor cleaner according to manufacturer's instructions. After cleaning, rinse in solvent and blow dry with compressed air. Make certain to use all parts in the overhaul kit to help eliminate unnecessary trouble.

Figure 38 is a sectional view of the single, dual throat, downdraft carburetor used on the early 1600 and 2002 models. **Figure 39** shows the 2002A carburetor. **Figure 40** is a sectional view of the dual sidedraft carburetor used on

the 2002ti. Figure 16 and **Figures 41 and 42** show the location of parts on the 32/32 DIDTA carburetor.

AIR CLEANER

Removal/Servicing

1. (*1600, 2002, 2002A*) See **Figure 43**. Pull off the hose from the intake preheater. Remove vacuum hose and loosen attachment nuts at the anti-vibration mountings. Remove air cleaner housing from carburetor and pull off the bleed hose. Clean the housing in suitable solvent. Make certain all air passages are open. Inspect and replace the air filter if dirty.

2. (*2002ti*) See **Figure 44**. Remove intake scoop at rear and pull off bleeder hose. Loosen hose clamp on hose leading to carburetor and remove hose. Unscrew the fixing bolts and remove the air cleaner. Clean all parts with suitable solvent.

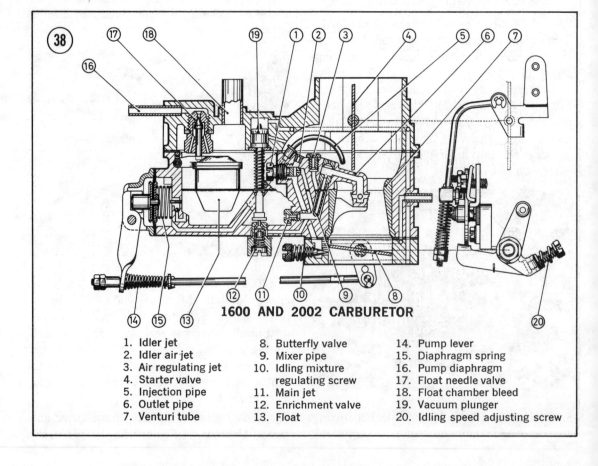

1600 AND 2002 CARBURETOR

1. Idler jet
2. Idler air jet
3. Air regulating jet
4. Starter valve
5. Injection pipe
6. Outlet pipe
7. Venturi tube
8. Butterfly valve
9. Mixer pipe
10. Idling mixture regulating screw
11. Main jet
12. Enrichment valve
13. Float
14. Pump lever
15. Diaphragm spring
16. Pump diaphragm
17. Float needle valve
18. Float chamber bleed
19. Vacuum plunger
20. Idling speed adjusting screw

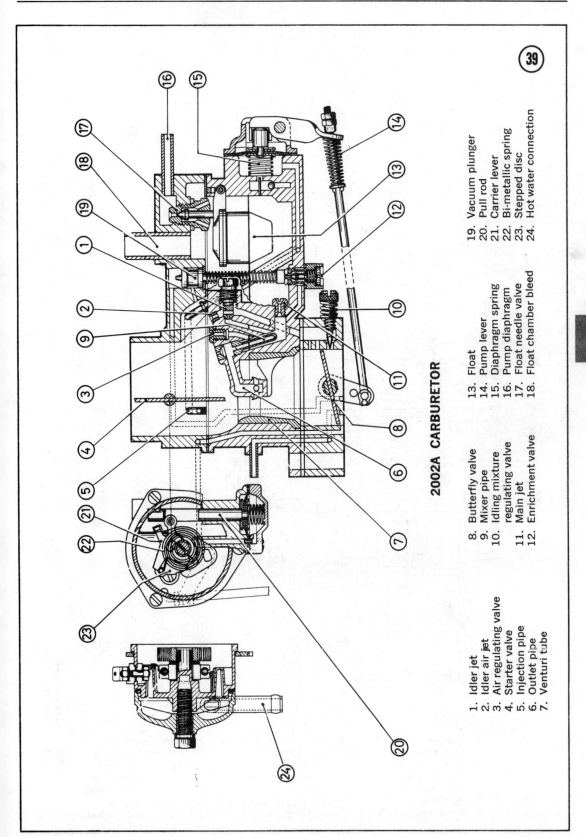

2002A CARBURETOR

1. Idler jet
2. Idler air jet
3. Air regulating valve
4. Starter valve
5. Injection pipe
6. Outlet pipe
7. Venturi tube

8. Butterfly valve
9. Mixer pipe
10. Idling mixture
    regulating valve
11. Main jet
12. Enrichment valve

13. Float
14. Pump lever
15. Diaphragm spring
16. Pump diaphragm
17. Float needle valve
18. Float chamber bleed

19. Vacuum plunger
20. Pull rod
21. Carrier lever
22. Bi-metallic spring
23. Stepped disc
24. Hot water connection

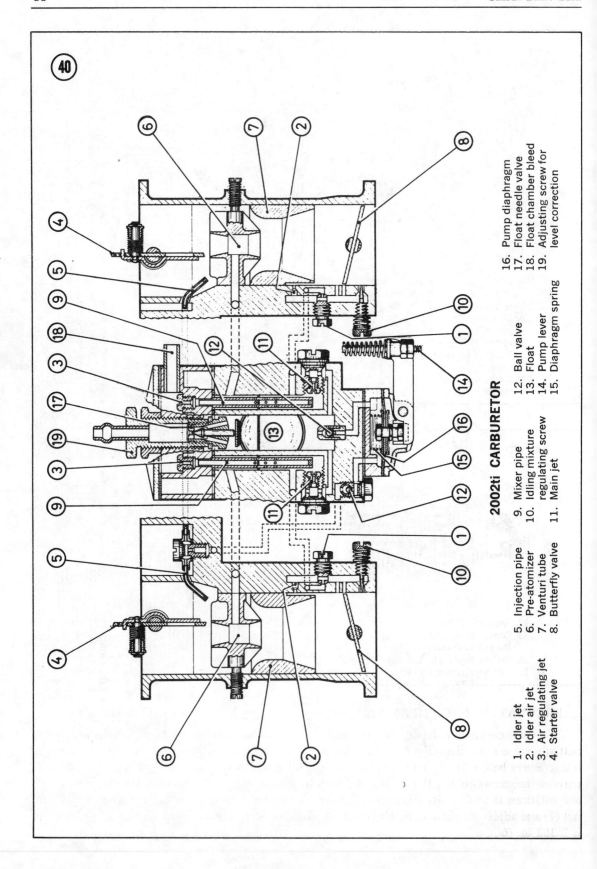

2002ti CARBURETOR

1. Idler jet
2. Idler air jet
3. Air regulating jet
4. Starter valve
5. Injection pipe
6. Pre-atomizer
7. Venturi tube
8. Butterfly valve
9. Mixer pipe
10. Idling mixture regulating screw
11. Main jet
12. Ball valve
13. Float
14. Pump lever
15. Diaphragm spring
16. Pump diaphragm
17. Float needle valve
18. Float chamber bleed
19. Adjusting screw for level correction

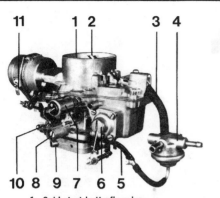

1. Cold start butterfly valve
2. Breather tube
3. Fuel inlet
4. Fuel return valve
5. Vacuum bore for distributor and return valve
6. Accelerator pump
7. Electromagnetic idling shut-off valve
8. Idle air by-pass control screw
9. Idling mixture control screw
10. Throttle valve adjusting screw (do not adjust)
11. Connection for electric heating of the automatic choke

④1

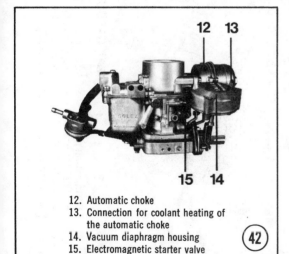

12. Automatic choke
13. Connection for coolant heating of the automatic choke
14. Vacuum diaphragm housing
15. Electromagnetic starter valve

④2

④3

④4

6

④5

PREHEATER BUTTERFLY VALVE

To avoid carburetor icing, the preheater butterfly valve must disengage from the stop at temperatures below 50°F. To adjust the valve, unscrew the screws holding the cover to the body and withdraw the valve. See **Figure 45**. Loosen nut (1) and adjust the valve until dimension (A) is 2.362 in. (60mm).

EXHAUST SYSTEM

The exhaust system consists of various pipes, brackets, connectors, and mufflers, as shown in **Figure 46** (typical). All parts are replaceable, but a cutting torch and welding device are usually required for removal of the mufflers from the exhaust pipes. Such service is usually done faster by a specialist in exhaust systems.

EXHAUST SYSTEM

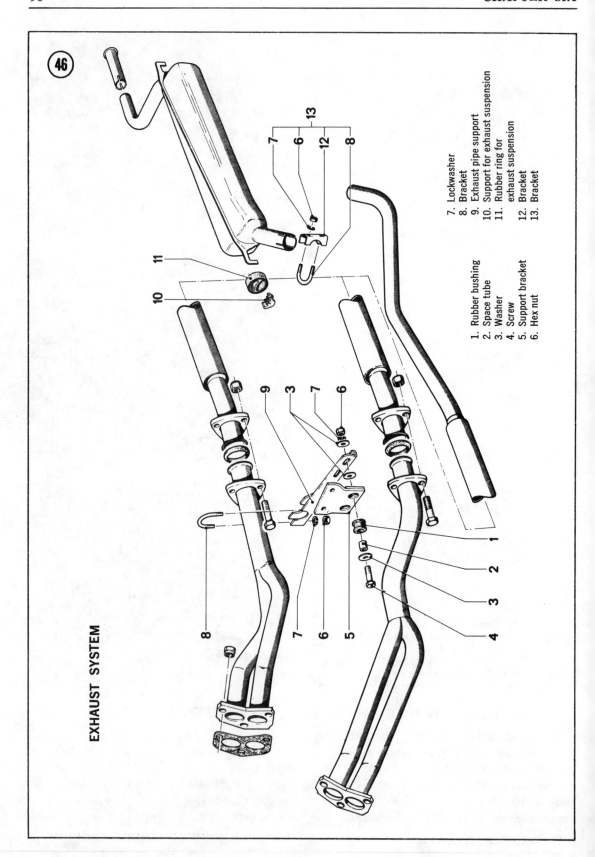

1. Rubber bushing
2. Space tube
3. Washer
4. Screw
5. Support bracket
6. Hex nut
7. Lockwasher
8. Bracket
9. Support for exhaust suspension
10. Support for exhaust suspension
11. Rubber ring for exhaust suspension
12. Bracket
13. Bracket

CHAPTER SEVEN

EMISSION CONTROL SYSTEM

Since 1968, all BMW's imported into the United States have incorporated emission-control devices to govern the release of hydrocarbons and carbon monoxide into the atmosphere. Over the years, the requirements have become more stringent. Therefore, several differences exist between models.

Figure 1 is a typical example of a closed emission control system. That is, vapors from the fuel tank and the crankcase are fed back to the engine for burning rather than being allowed to escape into the atmosphere. Additionally, fresh air flow is directed by a belt driven air pump to injector tubes located in each exhaust port immediately behind the exhaust valve. Since exhaust gases at this point are above ignition temperatures, mixture with an excess of oxygen is all that is required to start a burning action. This action burns the noxious hydrocarbons and changes most of the carbon monoxide to harmless carbon dioxide. The emission of nitrogen oxides is controlled by means of exhaust gas recycling.

Later models are equipped with an exhaust emission control system, instead of the closed emission control system described above. See **Figure 2**. This system essentially consists of a calibrated intake manifold for constant distribution of the air/fuel mixture to the cylinders and improved idle mixture, a carburetor with a reduced flow curve, and a thermal reactor with air injection.

The carburetor is equipped with a delay mechanism that holds the throttle valve slightly open during coasting.

The thermal reactor replaces the exhaust manifold. Fresh air is injected into the reactor to promote further burning of the exhaust gases by an air pump, via a diverter. Some of the exhaust gas is also recirculated to the intake manifold, where it is mixed with the air/fuel mixture for reburning. This gas is returned via a 2-stage exhaust gas recirculation (EGR) valve, which passes a small amount of exhaust gas during low engine loads, and a larger amount when the engine load is higher.

Later models are also equipped with an evaporation control system, consisting of a charcoal canister, a liquid-vapor separator, and purge lines.

The adjustments and services described below should be performed every 8,000 miles (12,500 miles on later models). Major service to the emission control system should be referred to a BMW dealer since it is complex and requires tools and skills not usually available to car owners.

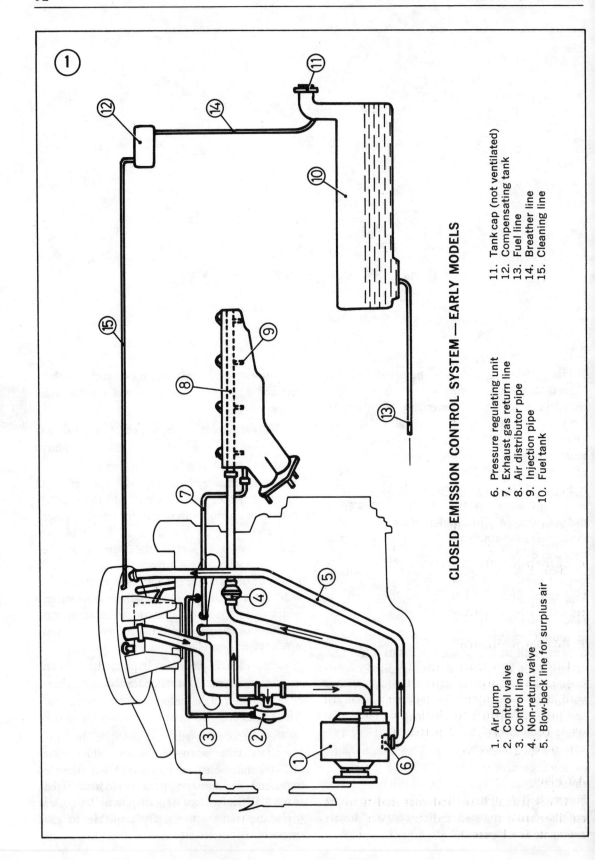

CLOSED EMISSION CONTROL SYSTEM — EARLY MODELS

1. Air pump
2. Control valve
3. Control line
4. Non-return valve
5. Blow-back line for surplus air

6. Pressure regulating unit
7. Exhaust gas return line
8. Air distributor pipe
9. Injection pipe
10. Fuel tank

11. Tank cap (not ventilated)
12. Compensating tank
13. Fuel line
14. Breather line
15. Cleaning line

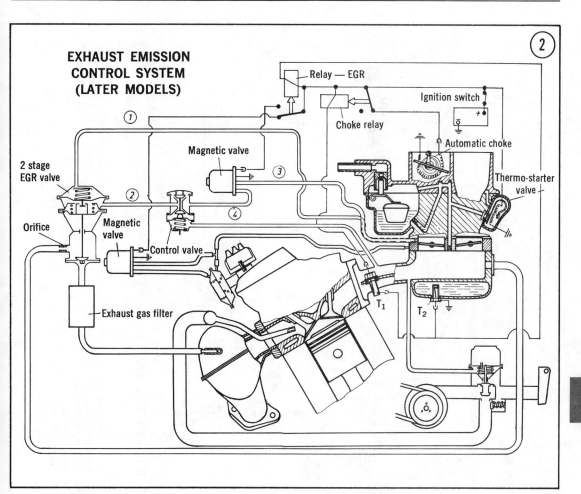

EXHAUST EMISSION
CONTROL SYSTEM
(LATER MODELS)

Relay — EGR

Ignition switch

Choke relay

①

Magnetic valve

③

Automatic choke

2 stage
EGR valve

②

Thermo-starter
valve

④

Orifice

Magnetic
valve

Control valve

Exhaust gas filter

T_1

T_2

Ignition Timing Adjustment

Tune and time the engine ignition system, using the procedures given in Chapter Four. The engine must be in good mechanical condition and tuned and timed to specifications for the emission control systems to be most effective.

Carburetor Adjustment

Using the procedure given in Chapter Four, connect an exhaust gas analyzer in accordance with the manufacturer's instructions and adjust the fuel/air mixture to obtain a carbon monoxide content of 0.8-1.2 percent (1.5-3.0 percent on early models).

Air Filter

1. Check that all hoses and lines leading to the air filter are connected and that all connectors are tight. See **Figure 3**.

2. Check condition of hoses and lines for deterioration. If defective, replace.

Pressure Regulating Valve

1. The pressure regulating valve (if so equipped) is located at the bottom of the air pump, as shown in **Figure 4**. Remove blow-back hose from pressure regulating valve.

2. Press palm of the hand lightly on the pressure regulating valve. The valve should open.

3. Connect a tachometer, start the engine, and check the pressure regulating valve for operation. It should open at 1,700-2,000 rpm.

4. If the valve opens at a speed of less than 1,700 rpm, the valve is defective and must be replaced. If the valve opens at a speed higher than 2,000 rpm, the air pump is defective and must be overhauled or replaced. Refer such service to your dealer.

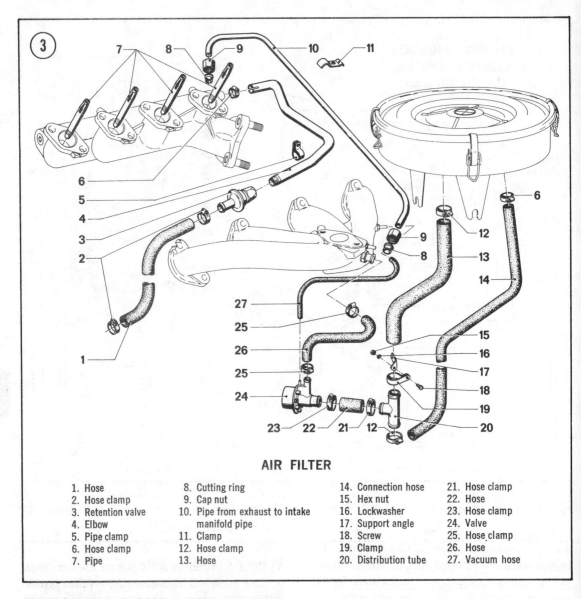

AIR FILTER

1. Hose	8. Cutting ring	14. Connection hose	21. Hose clamp
2. Hose clamp	9. Cap nut	15. Hex nut	22. Hose
3. Retention valve	10. Pipe from exhaust to intake	16. Lockwasher	23. Hose clamp
4. Elbow	manifold pipe	17. Support angle	24. Valve
5. Pipe clamp	11. Clamp	18. Screw	25. Hose clamp
6. Hose clamp	12. Hose clamp	19. Clamp	26. Hose
7. Pipe	13. Hose	20. Distribution tube	27. Vacuum hose

5. If the valve must be replaced with a new one, use 2 screwdrivers to pry the valve out of the pump housing.

Air Pump Servicing

Major overhaul and servicing of the air pump should be referred to a BMW dealer. **Figure 5** shows the details of the air pump and related parts.

1. Periodically inspect condition of drive belt and hoses. Check that belt tension is correct. When pushed in by thumb pressure, the belt should deflect 0.2-0.4 in. (5-10mm). If the belt

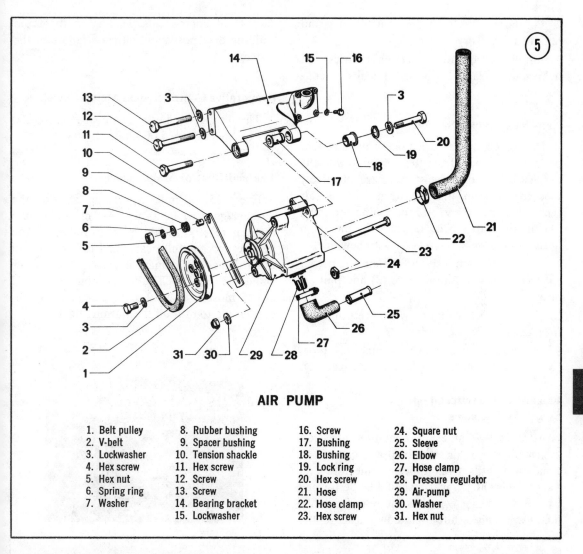

AIR PUMP

1. Belt pulley	8. Rubber bushing	16. Screw	24. Square nut
2. V-belt	9. Spacer bushing	17. Bushing	25. Sleeve
3. Lockwasher	10. Tension shackle	18. Bushing	26. Elbow
4. Hex screw	11. Hex screw	19. Lock ring	27. Hose clamp
5. Hex nut	12. Screw	20. Hex screw	28. Pressure regulator
6. Spring ring	13. Screw	21. Hose	29. Air-pump
7. Washer	14. Bearing bracket	22. Hose clamp	30. Washer
	15. Lockwasher	23. Hex screw	31. Hex nut

or hoses are defective, replace with new ones.

2. To adjust belt tension, loosen bolts on the mounting bracket pivots and tension shackle. Adjust the belt by moving the pump until the proper belt deflection is reached. Tighten the bolts securely.

3. To replace the belt, loosen the bolts on the pivots and the tension shackle, push the air pump toward engine, and remove belt from air pump and crankshaft pulley. Replace with new one and adjust as discussed above.

4. To remove the air pump, remove the bolts at the mounting bracket pivots and tension shackle. Remove drive belt from around pulley and withdraw pump from engine. To replace, reverse these steps and adjust drive belt tension.

5. With the pump removed, check the condition of the bushings in the mounting bracket pivots. If defective, remove snap ring at outside end of each pivot and remove bushing from mounting bracket.

Control Valve Servicing

A defective control valve is usually indicated when it is difficult to accurately set carburetor slow idle mixture at proper rpm and when there is backfiring in the exhaust when the throttle is closed. Should these conditions exist, replace the control valve with a new one.

1. See Figure 3. Loosen hose clamps (25, 23) from hoses attached to control valve (24).

2. Pull hoses (21, 26) from control valve and remove valve from engine.

3. Install new control valve, connect hoses, and tighten hose clamps. Check for leaks at connections.

Non-Return Valve Servicing

The non-return valve is a one-way valve that permits air to flow from the air pump into the exhaust manifold. Exhaust gases are effectively blocked from flowing backward into the air pump as long as the valve is operating correctly. Should the valve become stuck in the open position, remove it and replace with new one.

1. See Figure 3. Loosen hose clamp (2) from connection at non-return valve (3) and pull off hose (1).

2. Use a wrench to unscrew non-return valve from exhaust manifold pipe.

3. Install new valve to exhaust manifold pipe, connect hose, and tighten hose clamp securely.

Exhaust Gas Recirculation System Maintenance

After 25,000 miles of operation, the EGR system should be disassembled and cleaned to remove deposits from tubes, connectors and valves. This is a job which should be performed by a BMW dealer, who has the required tools. The use of makeshift tools could lead to the damage of components, leading to the rapid build-up of deposits and ultimate failure of the system.

Evaporative Control System Maintenance

The air cleaner in the charcoal filter should be replaced every 25,000 miles.

Thermal Reactor Maintenance

Every 25,000 miles a warning lamp on the dash (**Figure 6**) lights up. At this point, the thermal reactor should be removed from the vehicle and carefully examined for cracks and other damage. If damage is present, the reactor should be replaced. The contacts on the interval switch must be opened to reset the mileage recorder and to turn off the warning light.

CHAPTER EIGHT

COOLING SYSTEM

The cooling system consists of a pressurized radiator, thermostat, centrifugal-type water pump, fan, and necessary hoses. The passenger compartment heater is connected to the cooling system by hoses to supply hot water. The fan is mounted to the water pump and is driven by a belt and pulley from the crankshaft pulley. **Figure 1** is an exploded diagram of the system.

Cooling Circuit

The centrifugal pump, driven by a belt from the crankshaft, takes water from the radiator and delivers it through a hose to the engine block water jacket and then to the cylinder head. After leaving the cylinder head, the water passes through a hose to the top of the radiator. From the lower part of the radiator it returns through a hose to the pump, which delivers it once more to the cylinder block.

The thermostat, fitted next to the water pump in the water hose system, restricts the water circulation through the radiator until the water temperature is high enough for the engine to run properly. The thermostat valve begins to open at 176°F and is fully open when the temperature reaches 185°F. When the thermostat valve is closed, the water returns directly to the engine block through a passage in the cylinder head.

COOLING SYSTEM SERVICE

Draining Cooling System

1. Set heater control to HOT position and remove radiator filler cap.

2. Open drain cocks on cylinder block and bottom of radiator. If anti-freeze solution is being used, save the solution for reuse.

Filling Cooling System

1. Set heater control to HOT position and close radiator and cylinder block drain cocks. Remove radiator cap.

2. Fill radiator with clean water or anti-freeze solution.

3. Replace radiator cap, start engine, and bring it up to operating temperature so that the thermostat opens. Stop the engine and top up radiator with coolant.

Pressure Testing

Use a pressure tester, as shown in **Figure 2**, to test the cooling system.

1. Start engine and bring it up to operating temperature.

2. Remove radiator cap and top up radiator with coolant.

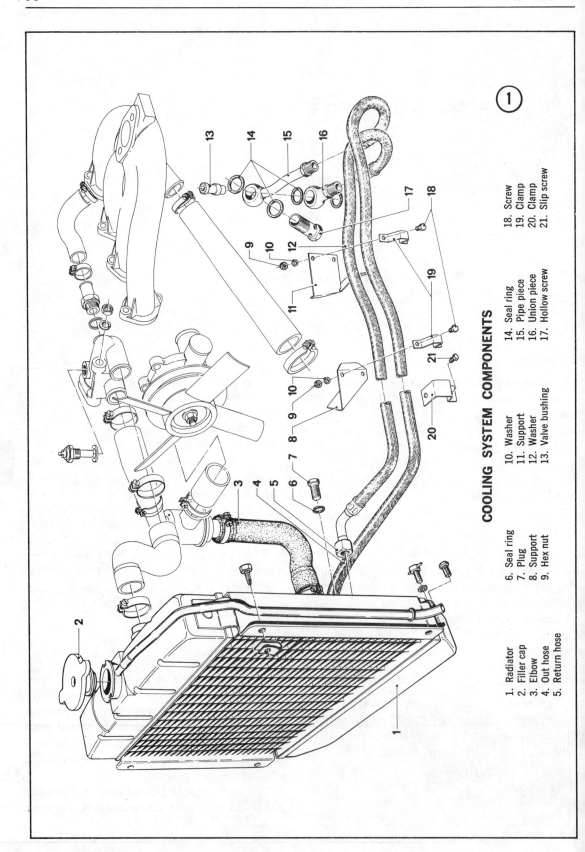

①

COOLING SYSTEM COMPONENTS

1. Radiator
2. Filler cap
3. Elbow
4. Out hose
5. Return hose

6. Seal ring
7. Plug
8. Support
9. Hex nut

10. Washer
11. Support
12. Washer
13. Valve bushing

14. Seal ring
15. Pipe piece
16. Union piece
17. Hollow screw

18. Screw
19. Clamp
20. Clamp
21. Slip screw

WARNING

Use care when removing radiator cap on a warm or hot engine. Hot water under pressure can cause severe scalding or burns. Loosen radiator cap to first notch and wait for pressure to escape before finally removing cap.

3. Fit the pressure tested to radiator filler neck.

4. Pump up the pressure to 14.7 lb./in.² The cooling system should maintain this pressure for at least 2 minutes.

5. A more severe test may be made by repeating the above steps, but with the engine running.

6. During testing, inspect all hoses, connections, and radiator for signs of leaks. Repair or replace defective parts.

7. Severe fluctuations of the tester readings without any sign of external leaks usually indicates a leaky cylinder head gasket.

8. Wash the radiator cap thoroughly to remove all traces of dirt, rust, or sediment. Connect the pressure tester to the radiator cap, as shown in **Figure 3**. Leave the cap wet.

9. Pump pressure up to 14 lb./in.² Discard radiator cap and replace with new one if it cannot hold the above pressure for at least 10 seconds. If it holds the pressure satisfactorily, pump the pressure up to 14.7 lb./in.² At this pressure, or slightly above, the pressure relief valve in the cap should open. If it does not, replace cap with new one.

Flushing Cooling System

1. Drain cooling system and remove both drain cocks.

2. Insert water hose into radiator filler and run water through the system until all signs of rust and sediment disappear.

3. Mount a water hose adaptor to radiator and/or cylinder block drain hole. Connect water hose to adaptor and run water backwards through the system until water runs clear.

4. Remove adaptor, replace drain cocks, and fill radiator with clean water or anti-freeze solution.

5. Warm up car until operating temperature is reached. Top up radiator with coolant.

Anti-Freeze Solution

To protect the cooling system and engine during cold weather, use an inhibited glycol base anti-freeze solution. Because of the searching effect of this solution, check the cooling system for leaks before and after adding anti-freeze. For the amount of solution required to safeguard the system at specific temperature ranges, follow manufacturer's instructions. The anti-freeze solution should be drained and discarded at least once a year.

THERMOSTAT

The thermostat should be removed, inspected, tested, and replaced as required if the engine runs hotter than normal or if it takes an excessive time to warm up. Overheating may be a symptom that the thermostat is stuck in the closed position. Failure of the engine to warm up in a normal time, might indicate the thermostat is stuck in the open position.

The thermostat is located next to the water pump and has 3 hoses connected to it, as shown in **Figure 4**.

8

Removal

1. Remove radiator cap and drain coolant below level of thermostat by opening drain cock at bottom of radiator.

2. See Figure 4. Loosen the hose clamps and disconnect the lower hose, water pump hose, and upper hose from thermostat. Remove thermostat unit.

Testing

1. Visually inspect for rust and corrosion. Check the bellows for deterioration and punctures. If obviously defective, replace with new one.

2. If the thermostat appears satisfactory, place it and a thermometer in a container of water. Heat thermostat and watch carefully for the valve to open. See **Figure 5**. The valve should start to open at 176°F. Measure the length of valve travel with a ruler. Full travel should be 0.315 in. (8mm).

3. Replace defective thermostat. Install using reverse procedures of removal.

RADIATOR

Removal/Replacement

1. Drain radiator by opening drain cock at bottom of radiator.

2. Unscrew screw at bottom left of the radiator. See **Figure 6**.

3. See **Figure 7**. Remove rubber hose from preheater housing. Disconnect preheater housing from intake air vent.

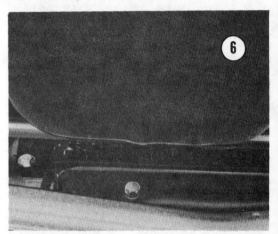

4. Disconnect upper and lower hoses from radiator. Disconnect overflow hose.

5. Unscrew hex head screws from front supports and lift the radiator upwards and out of the engine compartment.

6. To install, reverse above steps. Fill radiator with coolant. Start engine and bring up to normal operating temperature. Inspect all connections for leaks. Remove filler cap and top up radiator as required.

WATER PUMP

The water pump impeller and fan pulley hub are press fitted to the spindle, rather than being keyed. Disassembly requires a puller to remove the fan pulley hub and a press to remove the impeller and water pump bearing. For this reason, it may be easier to replace a defective pump with a new or rebuilt unit rather than disassemble and service it. **Figure 8** (next page) is an exploded view of the water pump.

Removal/Replacement

1. Drain the cooling system and remove the radiator as described above.

2. See **Figure 9**. Bend down tabs securing fan blade mounting bolts. Unscrew and remove bolts. Remove fan from fan pulley.

3. See **Figure 10**. Loosen alternator attaching bolts, push alternator towards block, and remove belt from pulleys. Remove fan pulley from fan pulley hub.

4. Loosen hose clamps and disconnect all hoses leading to water pump.

5. See **Figure 11**. Remove bolts and washers holding water pump to cylinder block. Separate water pump from cylinder block.

6. To replace, reverse the above steps. Use new gasket and washers.

Disassembly/Servicing

1. Remove water pump, as described above.

2. See **Figure 12**. Use a puller to withdraw the fan pulley hub from the spindle.

3. See **Figure 13**. Remove circlip (1) and spacer ring (2) from housing.

4. Use a press to remove the impeller from the spindle and the water pump bearing out of the housing.

5. See **Figure 14**. Knock out axial friction seal and lift out cover ring.

6. Clean all parts thoroughly. Remove scale from impeller and pump housing.

7. Inspect the pump housing for distortion, cracks, or splits. Replace if defective. With a

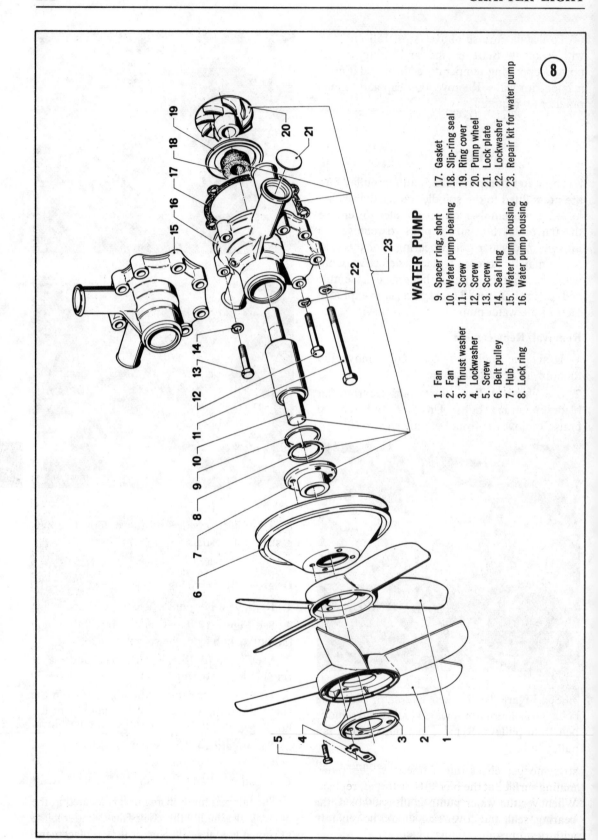

WATER PUMP

1. Fan
2. Fan
3. Thrust washer
4. Lockwasher
5. Screw
6. Belt pulley
7. Hub
8. Lock ring

9. Spacer ring, short
10. Water pump bearing
11. Screw
12. Screw
13. Screw
14. Seal ring
15. Water pump housing
16. Water pump housing

17. Gasket
18. Slip-ring seal
19. Ring cover
20. Pump wheel
21. Lock plate
22. Lockwasher
23. Repair kit for water pump

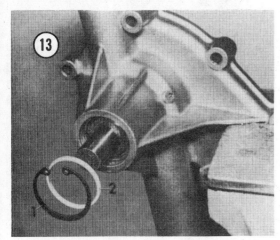

8. To assemble, reverse the steps used during disassembly. During assembly, the distance of the top of the fan pulley hub and the water pump should be 2.965 in. (75.3mm), as shown by (A) in **Figure 15**. Clearance between the impeller and the pump housing should be 0.039 in. (1mm), as shown in **Figure 16**. A press force of approximately 970 lb. is required to fit the spindle to the impeller and the bearing within the housing.

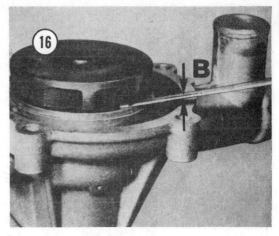

9. Install the water pump to the cylinder block. Use new washers and gasket.

TEMPERATURE SENSING UNIT

The temperature sensing unit is located in the housing attached to the side of the cylinder head, as shown in **Figure 17**. Repair is by replacement.

straightedge, check the flatness of the pump mating surface at the block. If distorted, replace. Whenever the water pump is disassembled, the bearing, seal, and cover ring should be replaced with new ones.

1. Remove electrical connector from top of temperature sensing unit.

2. Open radiator drain cock and drain coolant below level of housing.

3. Unscrew unit from housing and replace with new one. Use a new gasket at base of unit.

FAN BELT TENSION ADJUSTMENT

Proper adjustment of the fan belt is essential. If it is too tight, bearings in the water pump and alternator will wear quickly. If it is loose, the engine will tend to overheat and the alternator will not charge normally. To adjust the tension, proceed as follows:

1. See Figure 19 in Chapter Four. Loosen alternator fixing bolts on bracket and pivot.

2. Move the alternator to such a position that by pushing on the fan belt it deflects approximately 0.4 in. (10mm).

3. When adjusted, tighten all bolts and recheck deflection.

WATER HOSES

All water hoses, including heater hoses, should be inspected periodically for signs of leaks, cracks, or weakness. At the earliest sign of deterioration, a defective hose should be replaced.

CHAPTER NINE

ELECTRICAL SYSTEM

The electrical system consists of the battery, ignition/starter switch, starter motor, starter solenoid, distributor, alternator (generator), voltage regulator, and coil. The following sections provide details for removal, inspection, repair/replacement, and installation of these units.

BATTERY

Most models are equipped with a 12-volt negative ground battery and electrical system; early models have a 6-volt positive ground system. Typically, the battery is mounted within a holder on the left side of the engine compartment.

Inspection

1. Inspect the battery frequently for signs of corrosion on top of the battery and on the case. Use a solution of water and baking soda to neutarlize any corrosion and wipe the battery clean.
2. After cleaning, coat battery terminals lightly with Vaseline.
3. Inspect battery connections and battery cables for tightness and corrosion damage. Replace if defective.
4. Check battery condition with a hydrometer, as discussed in Chapter Four. If any of the cells are weak, recharge the battery. If recharging does not return the battery to satisfactory condition, replace it before trouble starts.

Replacement

1. Disconnect battery cables from battery terminals by loosening the bolts and spreading the connectors. Do not twist the cable around the battery poles as damage to the poles or insulation may result.
2. Loosen nuts from hold-down tie rods. Remove nuts and battery retaining clamp. Remove battery from battery holder. Make certain to note which cable belongs to the positive terminal and which belongs to the negative terminal.
3. Install new battery, battery retaining clamp, tie rods, and cables. Tighten all connections securely. Make certain the battery is full of electrolyte. Coat the battery terminals with Vaseline.

IGNITION/STARTER SWITCH

Maintenance of the ignition/starter switch is not required. Repair is made by replacement. **Figure 1** is an exploded diagram of the starter motor used on the 6-volt system; **Figure 2** the 12-volt system. Functionally, they are identical. The main differences are in the bushings and washers in the pinion gear drive.

9

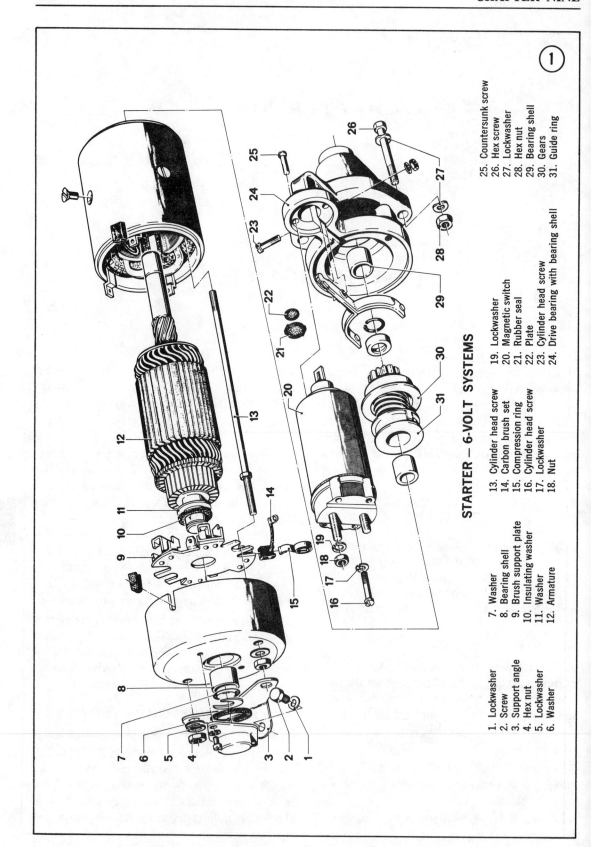

STARTER — 6-VOLT SYSTEMS

1. Lockwasher
2. Screw
3. Support angle
4. Hex nut
5. Lockwasher
6. Washer

7. Washer
8. Bearing shell
9. Brush support plate
10. Insulating washer
11. Washer
12. Armature

13. Cylinder head screw
14. Carbon brush set
15. Compression ring
16. Cylinder head screw
17. Lockwasher
18. Nut

19. Lockwasher
20. Magnetic switch
21. Rubber seal
22. Plate
23. Cylinder head screw
24. Drive bearing with bearing shell

25. Countersunk screw
26. Hex screw
27. Lockwasher
28. Hex nut
29. Bearing shell
30. Gears
31. Guide ring

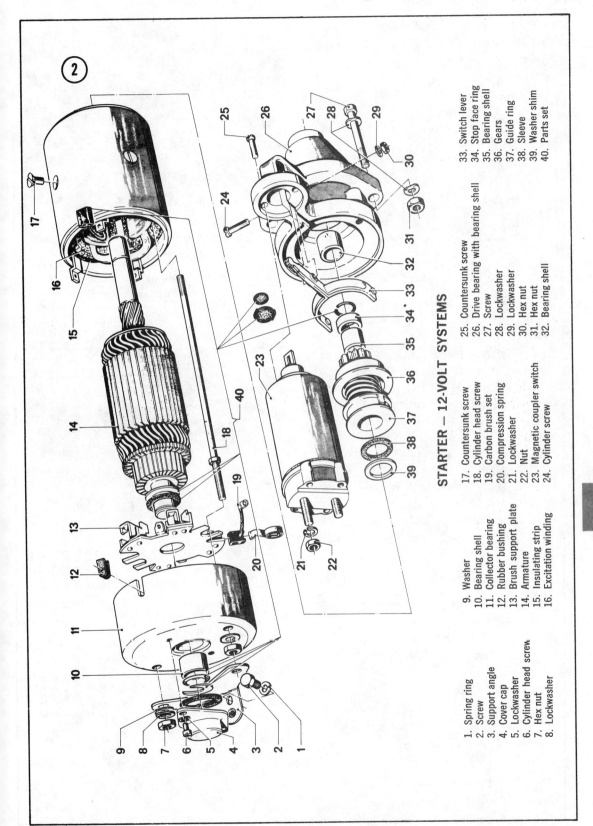

STARTER – 12-VOLT SYSTEMS

1. Spring ring
2. Screw
3. Support angle
4. Cover cap
5. Lockwasher
6. Cylinder head screw
7. Hex nut
8. Lockwasher
9. Washer
10. Bearing shell
11. Collector bearing
12. Rubber bushing
13. Brush support plate
14. Armature
15. Insulating strip
16. Excitation winding
17. Countersunk screw
18. Cylinder head screw
19. Carbon brush set
20. Compression spring
21. Lockwasher
22. Nut
23. Magnetic coupler switch
24. Cylinder screw
25. Countersunk screw
26. Drive bearing with bearing shell
27. Screw
28. Lockwasher
29. Lockwasher
30. Hex nut
31. Hex nut
32. Bearing shell
33. Switch lever
34. Stop face ring
35. Bearing shell
36. Gears
37. Guide ring
38. Sleeve
39. Washer shim
40. Parts set

9

Testing (Manual Transmission)

1. Connect voltmeter and ammeter, as shown in **Figure 3**.

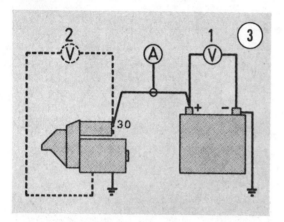

2. Place the gearshift in fourth gear and depress the footbrake.

3. Operate starter for 2-3 seconds and read meters. The voltmeter must drop below 8 volts (12-volt system) or 4.5 volts (6-volt system). Hook up the voltmeter as shown in circuit (2) and repeat test. Voltage reading should be the same as previously tested. If it is not, there is a poor ground connection on the starter motor or battery.

4. Current consumption, as shown on the ammeter, should be 25 to 35 amps.

5. For automatic transmission models, the starter must be removed from the car and the test performed on a bench.

Removal/Installation

1. See **Figure 4**. Disconnect negative battery terminal from battery.

2. Disconnect plug connections and supply cables from starter motor. Mark for later replacement.

3. Unscrew nuts holding starter motor to flywheel housing. Lift starter motor out of car.

4. To install, reverse the above steps. Tighten all connections.

Disassembly/Assembly

1. Unscrew cables to exciter winding. Remove bolts fixing solenoid to starter motor housing.

2. See **Figure 5**. Pull the solenoid out of the housing and detach the engaging lever, as shown.

3. See **Figure 6**. Unscrew screws fixing dust cap (1) to housing. Remove dust cap. Remove lockwasher (2), shims (3), and gasket (4).

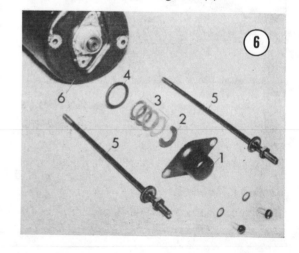

4. Unscrew and remove pole casing bolts (5) and pull off cap (6). Check the bushing in the cap for wear and damage.

5. Lift out positive brushes and remove brush support plate, as shown in **Figure 7**. Separate pole casing from armature by pulling it off.

6. See **Figure 8**. Unscrew and remove engaging lever bolt. Remove armature and engaging lever from end housing.

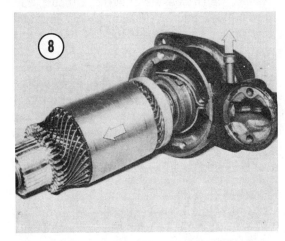

7. See **Figure 9**. Push thrust ring (1) backward, lift out retaining ring (2), and pull off starter gear. Pull thrust ring over the retaining ring. During assembly, coat coarse thread and starting ring with silicone lubricant.

8. To assemble, reverse the above steps.

Renewing Carbon Brushes

1. Check condition of the carbon brushes. If cracked or worn, replace with new ones. As a

matter of good practice, replace the brushes whenever the starter motor is disassembled.

2. Unsolder brush connections from brush support plate and remove brushes from holder. Install new brushes into holder and solder connections. Be careful that the springs do not snap hard against the brushes, as damage may result.

Overhauling

1. Use a test lamp to check the commutator and field coil, as shown in **Figure 10**. Sequentially place a test probe on each of the commutator segments and the other on the field coil. If the lamp lights, there is a short and the armature must be rebuilt or replaced.

2. Hook up an ammeter, as shown in **Figure 11**. Test voltage should be 2-4 volts. Check each commutator segment by moving the probe from

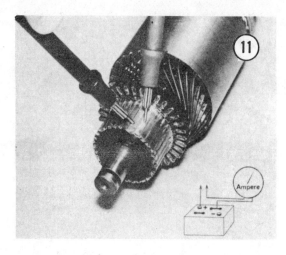

point-to-point. Deflection (amps) on the ammeter should be the same between segments. Large variations indicate an open in the circuit. The armature must be replaced.

3. Use a test lamp to check the exciter (pole) winding for ground. Place one probe on the starter motor housing and the other on the exciter winding wire contact connection. If the lamp lights, there is a short and the exciter windings must be replaced.

4. Check condition of the commutator segments for burns and distortion. Use an outside caliper to check the diameter of the commutator. It must not be less than 1.30 in. (33mm). If the minimum diameter has not been reached, the commutator can be lightly skimmed in a lathe to restore the surface to good condition.

5. After skimming, undercut mica between commutator segments to a depth of 0.02 in. (0.5mm), as shown in **Figure 12.**

6. Check the condition of bushings (bearings) at each end of the armature shaft. If defective, press them out and install new bushings with a drift. Soak new bushings in engine oil for ½ hour before installing.

7. To renew the exciter windings, mark the pole shoes so that they can be replaced in the same position. With a large screwdriver, remove screws holding exciter windings in the housing. Pull the exciter windings out of the housing.

8. Inspect the windings for wear and damage. If defective or if they tested as being grounded, replace with new ones. During installation, make certain to install the paper insulating strip between the windings and the housing. Before finally tightening pole screws, align pole shoes exactly parallel to the longitudinal axis of the housing. When installing the armature, make certain it does not drag on the windings and that it rotates freely.

DISTRIBUTOR

The distributor is the heart of the ignition system, which consists of the distributor, contact breaker points, condenser, coil, high and low tension circuit parts. The low tension (primary) consists of the power source (battery), contact breaker points, condenser, and primary winding of ignition coil. The high tension (secondary) circuit consists of ignition coil secondary winding, rotor arm, distributor cap electrical contacts, high tension cables, and spark plugs.

Mechanically, the distributor is driven off of the camshaft through gearing. **Figure 13** is an exploded view of the distributor.

Most of the trouble encountered in the distributor will be in the cap, rotor, contact points, condenser, or wiring. The distributor should not make any noise while the engine is running. If noises are apparent, either the bearings or gears are worn and should be replaced. Unless it is essential to remove the distributor from the engine for disassembly and part replacement, all services can be performed with the distributor in place. The contact points should be serviced and replaced periodically, as specified in Chapter Four. Replace the rotor and condenser whenever the contact points are replaced.

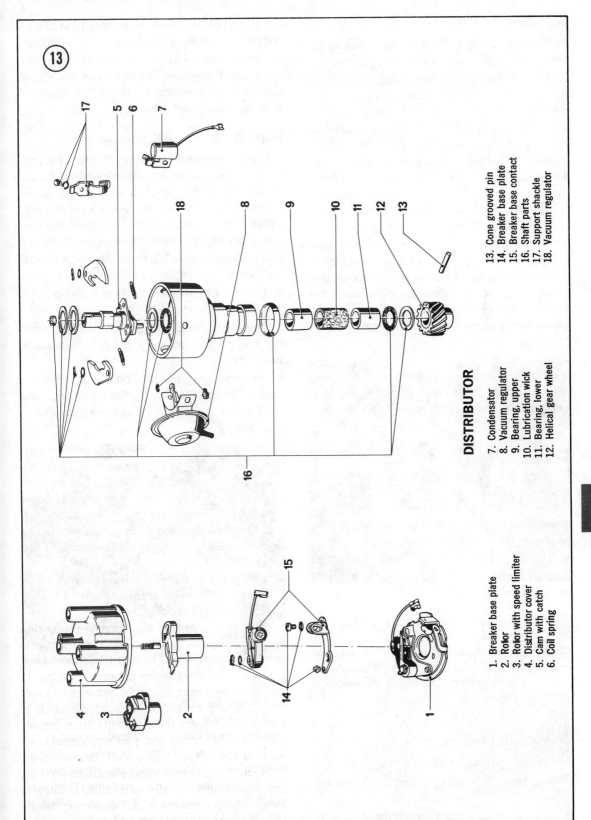

DISTRIBUTOR

1. Breaker base plate
2. Rotor
3. Rotor with speed limiter
4. Distributor cover
5. Cam with catch
6. Coil spring

7. Condensator
8. Vacuum regulator
9. Bearing, upper
10. Lubrication wick
11. Bearing, lower
12. Helical gear wheel

13. Cone grooved pin
14. Breaker base plate
15. Breaker base contact
16. Shaft parts
17. Support shackle
18. Vacuum regulator

9

Contact Point Adjustment

1. Unsnap the hold down clamps holding the distributor cap to the distributor.

2. Remove rotor by pulling it off the distributor shaft. Once the rotor is removed, the contact point assembly can be adjusted.

3. Rotate distributor cam by turning crankshaft pulley until the moving contact (rubbing arm) is positioned at the highest point on a cam lobe. The contact points should be open. Use a feeler gauge to measure the gap between the movable and stationary contact points. For correct gap, refer to Chapter Four.

4. See **Figure 14**. Loosen screw (2) and move the points until the correct gap is achieved. Tighten the screw. The feeler gauge should have a slight drag as it is moved back and forth, but you should not be able to see the contact point move. Recheck the gap after tightening screw. If incorrect, readjust.

NOTE: *The contact mating surfaces should have a grey frosted appearance. If the surfaces are partly worn, clean with a point file as required. If excessively worn, pitted, or burned, replace them.*

Contact Point Replacement

1. Remove distributor cap.

2. See Figure 14. Remove flat plug (1), unscrew screw (2), and lift out contact points.

3. When installing, make certain the shaft at the spring end fits into hole in the base plate. Reinstall screw and flat plug.

4. Adjust the points as described above. Make certain that the point surfaces mate exactly. If not, bend the movable contact point arm until they meet flatly and exactly.

Distributor Removal/Replacement

Unless complete disassembly of the distributor is necessary, do not loosen clamp bolt at base of distributor. Engine timing may be affected. Before removal, mark the position of the distributor base relative to the cylinder head so that it can be replaced in the same position.

1. Disconnect spark plug wires from distributor cap. Mark them for later replacement.

2. Unsnap the hold-down clamps and remove the distributor cap.

3. Disconnect wire lead on outside of distributor. Pull off the vacuum line from the vacuum advance can.

4. Set piston No. 1 to TDC on the compression stroke. The notch on the distributor rotor should line up with notch on distributor body, as shown in **Figure 15**.

5. Loosen the clamp bolt at the base of the distributor and pull up on the distributor until it comes out of the cylinder head housing.

6. To install, reverse the above steps. During installation, turn distributor rotor approximately 1.4 in. (35mm) counterclockwise from the notch in the distributor body, as shown in **Figure 16**. Insert distributor shaft into housing

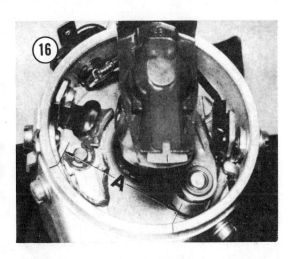

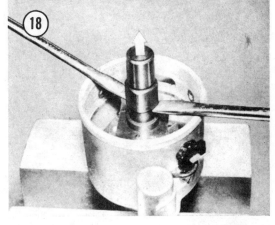

until gear meshes with gear on camshaft. When installed, the rotor mark and mark on distributor body should be lined up. The reference marks made at the base of the distributor should also line up. Tighten the base bolt securely.

Overhauling

1. See Figure 13 and proceed as follows:

2. Remove distributor.

3. Remove cap and rotor.

4. Remove vacuum unit by unscrewing screws holding it to the distributor, as shown in **Figure 17**. Remove contact breaker plate. Unscrew screw and remove condenser.

5. See **Figure 18**. Place distributor in vise equipped with soft jaws. With 2 screwdrivers, force cam upward until retaining ring springs

out of groove. Do not pull out felt or retaining ring underneath will spring out.

6. Use a 0.118 in. (3mm) diameter drill to drill out the grooved dowel pin located just above the drive gear.

7. See **Figure 19**. Remove distributor shaft with centrifugal weights and cam. Remove thrust washers (1) and insulating washers (2).

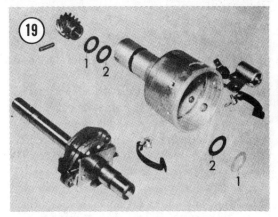

8. See **Figure 20**. Detach springs (2), withdraw grease felt (3), retaining ring (4), washer (5), and cam. Remove clips (6) and centrifugal weights (7). During assembly, lubricate cam with engine oil and centrifugal weights with light grease. If holder or springs are replaced, check centrifugal advance curve.

9. Check condition of bushings inside housing. If they are worn or damaged, drive out with suitable drift and install new ones.

10. Inspect all parts for wear and damage. Pay

special attention to condition of thrust washers, spacers, bearings, shaft, and springs. Replace parts as required. Visual wear or damage is sufficient cause to replace a part.

ALTERNATOR/GENERATOR

Some models are equipped with an alternator; some with a generator.

Alternator Description

The alternator is a self-rectifying, three-phase current generator consisting of the stationary armature (stator), rotating field (rotor), and a three-phase rectifying bridge of silicon diodes. The alternator generates alternating current and the silicon diodes convert the alternating to direct current for use in the car's electrical circuits. The output of the alternator is regulated by a voltage regulator to keep the battery in a satisfactory charged condition. The alternator is mounted at the front left side of the engine and is driven by a belt off of the crankshaft pulley. **Figure 21** (next page) is an exploded view.

To prevent damage to the diodes, the following general precautions should be observed.

1. Disconnect the leads between the battery, alternator, and regulator only when the ignition switch is turned off.

2. If the battery is to be charged in the car, disconnect the battery positive and negative leads.

3. If arc welding is to be done to any part of the car, connect the arc welder ground terminal directly to the car body.

Removal/Installation

1. Disconnect battery negative cable.

2. Pull off plug from alternator connection.

3. Remove cables from alternator.

4. Loosen bolts holding alternator to mounting bracket and pivot.

5. Push alternator toward engine block to loosen belt.

6. Remove belt from around pulley.

7. Remove bolts holding alternator to mounting bracket and pivot. Remove alternator from engine.

8. To replace, reverse the above steps. Make certain to install the belt so that it will deflect approximately 0.4 in. (10mm) when pushed in under thumb pressure.

Overhauling

General overhaul should be restricted to brush and bearing replacement. Service to the rotor assembly, stator, and diode assembly should be referred to your BMW dealer or automotive electric shop.

Brush Replacement

1. See **Figure 22**. Remove screws fixing end bearing housing to alternator housing. Remove end bearing housing and rotor from alternator housing.

2. Remove diode carrier by pulling off plug connections, as shown in **Figure 23**. Unscrew carbon brush holder fixing screws.

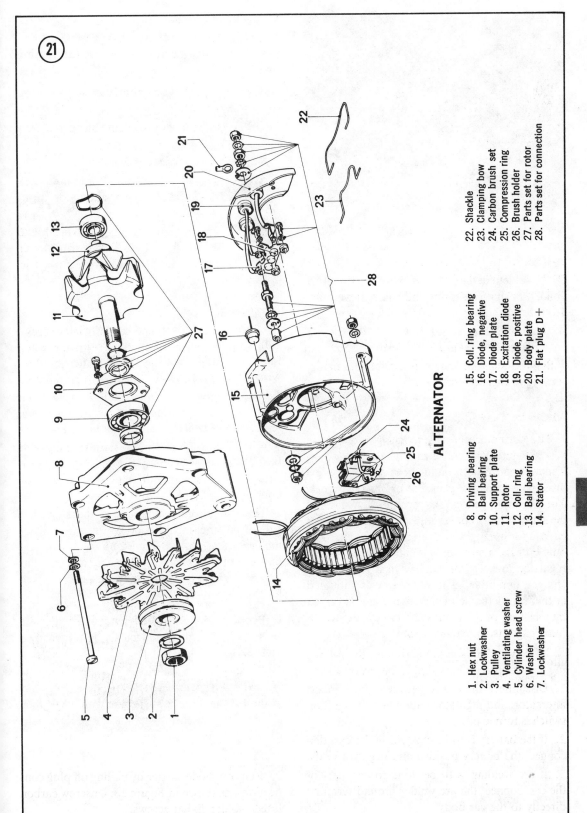

ALTERNATOR

1. Hex nut
2. Lockwasher
3. Pulley
4. Ventilating washer
5. Cylinder head screw
6. Washer
7. Lockwasher

8. Driving bearing
9. Ball bearing
10. Support plate
11. Rotor
12. Coll. ring
13. Ball bearing
14. Stator

15. Coll. ring bearing
16. Diode, negative
17. Diode plate
18. Excitation diode
19. Diode, positive
20. Body plate
21. Flat plug D+

22. Shackle
23. Clamping bow
24. Carbon brush set
25. Compression ring
26. Brush holder
27. Parts set for rotor
28. Parts set for connection

9

3. Unsolder carbon brush wire from brush holder. Push up on spring end and remove brush from brush holder.

4. Insert new brush inside holder, solder the lead into place, and secure the brush as shown in **Figure 24**.

5. Assemble the alternator, push the brushes into contact onto the rotor slip rings and secure the spring over the top of the brush.

Bearing Replacement

1. Secure the alternator in a vise equipped with soft jaws to prevent damage. Lock the fan pulley so that it cannot rotate.

2. Remove hex nut fixing pulley to shaft. Remove pulley, washer, and cooling vane from shaft.

3. See **Figure 25**. Remove spacer (1), press out rotor (2), and unscrew retainer plate (3). Press the grooved ball bearing (4) out of the bearing plate (5).

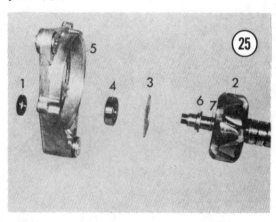

4. During installation, lubricate the ball bearing with suitable grease. The open side of bearing faces the armature. Push face plate (6) over wire retainer (7).

5. Use a press to remove ball bearing from armature shaft. Lubricate and install with press. Open side of bearing faces armature. Make certain to place corrugated washer in housing before the ball bearing.

Generator Overhauling

The generator is mounted at the front left side of the engine and is driven by a belt off of the crankshaft pulley. **Figure 26** is an exploded diagram of the generator. Removal and installation procedures are essentially the same as given for the alternator.

1. Place generator in vise equipped with soft jaws to prevent damage to housing. See Figure 26.

2. Remove screw securing cover strip to housing. With the cover strip removed, the condition of the brushes can be inspected without further disassembly by lifting up on the springs and withdrawing the brushes from the holders. If defective or badly worn, unscrew screws holding brush connectors to brush holder plate and remove brushes. Replace with new ones and connect wires. Be careful not to let the brushes snap against the armature due to spring pressure.

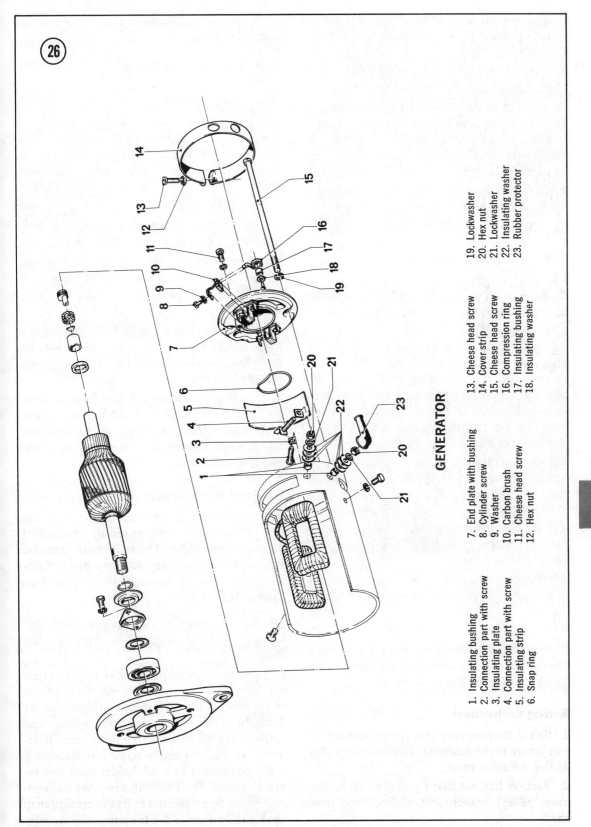

GENERATOR

1. Insulating bushing
2. Connection part with screw
3. Insulating plate
4. Connection part with screw
5. Insulating strip
6. Snap ring
7. End plate with bushing
8. Cylinder screw
9. Washer
10. Carbon brush
11. Cheese head screw
12. Hex nut
13. Cheese head screw
14. Cover strip
15. Cheese head screw
16. Compression ring
17. Insulating bushing
18. Insulating washer
19. Lockwasher
20. Hex nut
21. Lockwasher
22. Insulating washer
23. Rubber protector

9

3. Remove nut and washer holding pulley to armature shaft. This may require the use of an impact-type wrench.

4. Remove pulley, cooling fan, and key from shaft. Remove generator from vise.

5. Unscrew and remove through bolts holding the 2 end pieces to generator housing. Gently pull off the end piece partway, holding the brushes, until the brushes and springs can be seen.

6. Lift up both brushes by pushing against the spring. When the brushes are clear of the armatur, finish removing the end piece.

7. Gently pull the armature out of the housing. Take care not to drag the armature against the field windings.

8. Remove snap ring from shaft at retaining collar. Remove end piece when the armature shaft is clear of the bearing.

9. To remove the field windings, disconnect the wires at the pole connections and remove screws holding field windings to housing. The use of a wheel-operated screwdriver may be required. Remove field windings from housing. Take care not to damage the insulation between the windings and the housing.

10. On the brush end piece, remove seal on armature side. Press out the bushing and remove final seal. When installing new bushing, soak thoroughly in oil before pressing into place.

11. At the pulley end piece, remove bearing retainer screws. Remove retainer, bearing, and seals from housing.

12. Inspect all parts for wear or damage. Repair is by replacement, as discussed below. Always replace seals, bearing, bushing, and brushes with new ones whenever alternator is disassembled.

Brush Inspection/Replacement

1. Clean brushes and holders with suitable solvent.

2. Ensure that the brushes move freely in the holders. If required, lightly polish holder sides with fine glasspaper or file.

3. If brushes are badly worn, replace them with new ones.

4. Inspect springs for damage or weakness. Replace if defective.

Armature Inspection/Repair

1. Clean armature with suitable solvent on a clean cloth.

2. Clear insulation slots of copper and carbon residue. If the unit is in good condition, it will be smooth and free from pits or burned spots. Polish with fine glasspaper; do not use emery cloth.

3. Use a dial indicator to check runout of the armature. Maximum permissible runout is 0.0004 in. (0.01mm).

4. If the runout is excessive or the armature is badly worn, skim it with a lathe and cutting tool. Remove no more metal than absolutely necessary.

5. After skimming, undercut the insulators to a depth of 0.039 in. (1mm).

6. Polish with fine glasspaper, and clean with solvent.

Field Winding Continuity Testing

1. Connect ohmmeter between field connector and housing. Ohmmeter reading should be between 7 to 8 ohms.

2. If ohmmeter reading is "infinity", there is an open circuit in the field winding. Repair is by replacement.

3. If the reading is much below the specified level, the insulation of one field winding is defective. Repair is by replacement.

Armature Testing

1. To test for grounded armature, place one test lead of an ohmmeter on the armature shaft. Place other test lead on each commutator bar, one at a time. If continuity occurs on any bar, the armature is grounded and must be replaced.

2. Check the armature for opens. These are usually indicated by burn marks between the commutator bars and are caused by the brushes bridging the open circuit. Repair is by replacement.

3. To check the armature winding for shorts, mount the armature in a growler tester, as shown in **Figure 27**. Turn the growler on and hold a

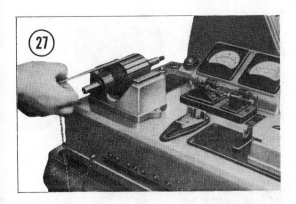

hacksaw blade slightly above, but not touching, the armature. Rotate the armature slowly. If the blade vibrates and is attracted to the armature, a winding is shorted. Repair is by replacement.

REGULATOR UNIT

Figure 28 shows the location and mounting screws of the regulator. Yellow adhesive tape around the bottom indicates a non-suppressed unit; white tape indicates a suppressed unit. The regulator unit regulates the generator output of voltage and amperage. A cut-out is also included to prevent overcharging of the battery and lamp damage.

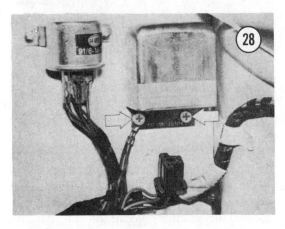

Due to the complexity of the regulator unit and the need for specialized tools and test equipment, service and adjusting of the regulator unit should be referred to your dealer.

IGNITION COIL

The ignition coil is connected to the distributor with high tension and low tension wires and to the car's wiring system. If faults are isolated to a defective coil, the coil must be replaced. To remove and install, disconnect wires leading to coil, unscrew and remove fixing screws, and install new coil. When installing, make certain to observe the proper polarity when connecting to the harness wire and the distributor low tension wire.

BODY
ELECTRICAL SYSTEM

This section covers the body electrical system. Information is given on the fuses, headlights, parking lights, signalling devices, taillights, windshield wiper motor, and heater motor. Wiring diagrams are included at the end of this chapter.

FUSES

Whenever a failure occurs in any part of the electrical system, always check the fuse box to see if a fuse has blown. If one has, it will be evident by blackening of the fuse or by a break of the metal element within the fuse. Usually the trouble is a short circuit in the wiring. This may be caused by worn-through insulation or by a wire which works its way loose and shorts to ground. Carry several spare fuses of proper amperage rating in the car.

Before replacing a fuse, determine what caused it to blow and correct the trouble. Never replace a fuse with one of a higher amperage rating than originally used. Never use tinfoil or other material to jump across fuse terminals. Failure to follow these basic rules could result in fire or damage to major parts, or loss of the entire car. By following the wiring diagrams at the end of the chapter, the circuits protected by each fuse can be determined.

Two different fuse boxes have been used. One contains 6 fuses and the other 12. A typical installation is shown in **Figure 29**. The fuse amperage and the circuits protected are given on the instruction sheet placed next to the fuse box. To replace or inspect fuses, remove the cover and inspect condition of metal element within the glass tube. If defective, remove fuse from the end clips and replace with new one.

9

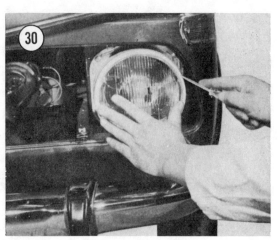

HEADLIGHTS

The headlights are of the sealed-beam replaceable type. Both the high beam and low beam circuits and filaments are included in one unit. Failure of one circuit requires replacement of the entire sealed-beam unit.

Removal/Replacement

1. If a headlight fails, check to see that both the high and low beam fail to operate. If they are both out, check the connector at the back of the unit to see that it is connected.

2. Check the fuse protecting the headlight circuit. If it is not damaged, replace the sealed-beam unit with a new one.

3. Remove front side radiator grille.

4. From inside front of fender, disconnect the connector from the sealed-beam unit.

5. See **Figure 30**. Remove screws fixing sealed-beam unit to holder and remove unit.

6. Install new unit by reversing above procedure. Have headlights adjusted by a BMW dealer or headlight specialist.

PARKING AND TURN INDICATOR LIGHTS

In early models, the parking lights were included as part of the headlight assembly. In later models, the parking and turn indicator lights are in the turn indicator assembly. Removal and replacement of the parking lights in the early models requires removal of the bulb holder from the back side of the headlight assembly, pushing in and turning the bulb in the holder, and removal of the bulb. Access to the holder is through the opening at the front of the fender.

On late models, remove screws fixing lens to housing, as shown in **Figure 31**. Pull out lens from housing; the bulb holder is part of the lens assembly. Remove and replace bulb.

TAILLIGHT ASSEMBLY

The taillight assembly includes the reverse light, taillight, turn indicator light, stoplight, and the common ground wire. Removal and replacement is done from inside the trunk.

1. See **Figure 32**. Open trunk and unscrew knurled knobs from fixing studs. Pull off hub holder housing.

2. Remove defective bulb and replace. In **Figure 33** (1) is the reverse light, (2) is the taillight, (3) the turn indicator, (4) the stoplight, and (5) the ground wire.

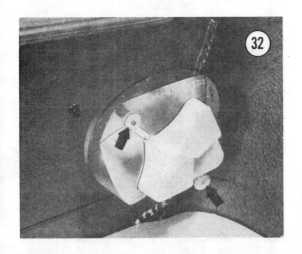

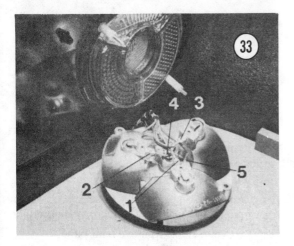

LICENSE PLATE LIGHT

See **Figure 34**. Remove screws fixing lens assembly to housing, remove lens assembly, disconect bulb from holder, and install new bulb.

INTERIOR LIGHT

See **Figure 35**. Use a screwdriver to press the light assembly out of the holder. Remove and replace bulb.

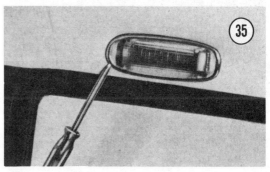

WINDSHIELD WIPER MOTOR

Removal/Installation

1. See **Figure 36**. Unscrew nut and remove drive crank from motor.

2. Unscrew bolts fixing motor to bracket.

3. See **Figure 37**. Disconnect cable (1) from connection. Loosen screw and disconnect ground wire (2).

4. Lift out windshield wiper motor. Repair is by replacement with new or rebuilt unit.

HEATER MOTOR

Removal/Installation

1. Disconnect battery negative cable.

2. Move heater control to WARM and drain coolant from radiator.

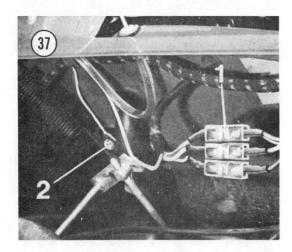

3. At the fire wall, loosen hose clamp on water return hose and disconnect hose.

4. See **Figure 38**. Detach feed hose (1) at water valve (2). Check condition of water valve and replace with new one if defective.

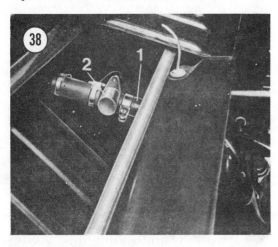

5. From inside car, remove screws holding storage tray and remove tray.

6. Remove screws holding lower center trim panel and remove panel.

7. Remove screws from outer left-hand trim panel and remove panel.

8. See **Figure 39**. Loosen screws and remove upper section of case.

9. On the control panel, remove control knobs by pulling off. Loosen and remove inner and outer screws fixing control panel in place. Remove control panel. Loosen cable clamps and disconnect clamps from control levers.

10. Release screws on either side of control levers.

11. Pull out ashtray. Pull off control lever knob and loosen screws at both ends of control lever panel. Remove panel. Remove 2 screws in back of panel.

12. Pull off electrical cable connections.

13. Remove nut and bolt fixing left-hand side of heater. Open glove compartment and remove nut and bolt fixing right-hand side of heater.

14. Pull off left-hand hot air hose.

15. Remove screws fixing trim panel beneath glove compartment. Remove trim panel.

16. Pull off right-hand hot air hose and carefully lift out heater.

17. Drill out rivets fixing heater cover. Remove clamps at rear of heater housing. Remove housing.

18. See **Figure 40**. Loosen hose clamp (1), clamp screw (2), screw (3), and retaining screws (4).

19. Remove rubber sleeves on either side of blower.

20. Pull off cables from back of blower motor. Detach cable from heater valve.

21. Disconnect cables from heater housing.

22. See **Figure 41**. Remove clamps and take out motor with fan downward. The motor and fan are balanced as an assembly. Do not separate fan from motor shaft.

23. Repair of the motor is by replacement with new or rebuilt assembly.

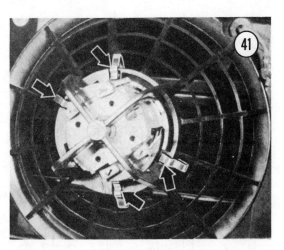

WIRING DIAGRAMS

The following wiring diagrams are provided as an aid in troubleshooting and maintenance of the electrical system. A diagram is provided for each of the 12-volt models, including the automatic transmission model.

9

WIRING DIAGRAM — 1600

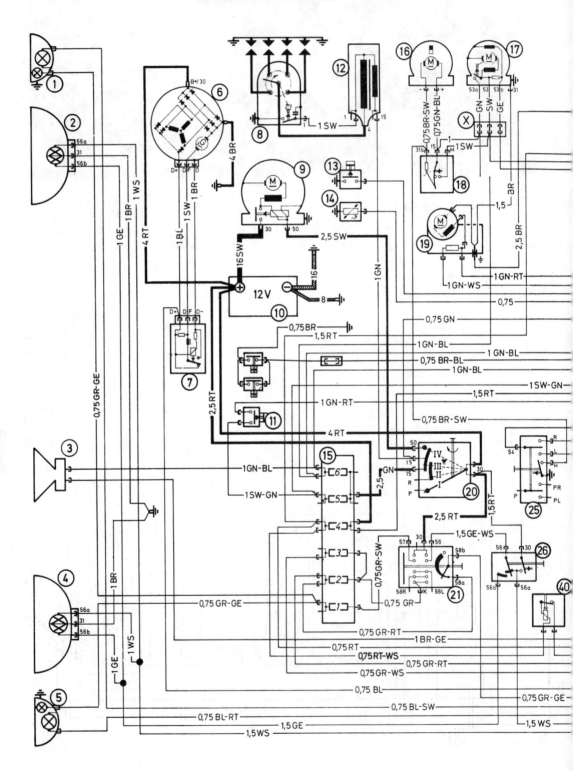

See Key on Page 126

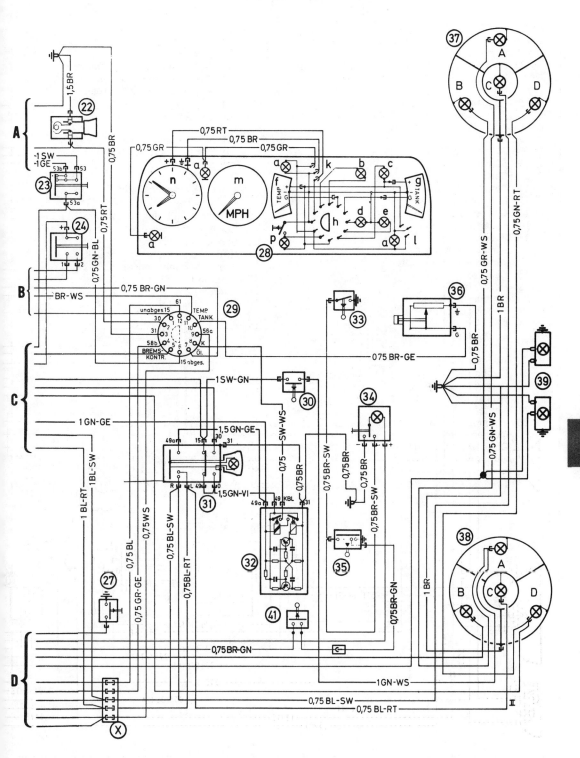

See Key on Page 126

KEY TO
WIRING DIAGRAM — 1600
(See Pages 124-125)

1. Turn indicator, front RH with parking light
2. Headlight, RH
3. Horn
4. Headlight, LH
5. Turn indicator, front LH with parking light
6. Alternator
7. Regulator
8. Distributor
9. Starter
10. Battery
11. Stop light switch
12. Ignition coil
13. Oil pressure switch
14. Remote thermometer sensor
15. Fuse box
16. Windshield washer pump
17. Windshield wiper motor
18. Delay relay
19. Heater blower
20. Ignition/starter switch
    Switch positions:
    I   Stop
    II Garage
    III Drive
    IV Start
21. Light switch
22. Cigarette lighter
23. Windshield wiper switch
24. Heater switch
25. Turn indicator and windshield
    washer switch
26. Dimmer with flasher unit
27. Horn ring
28. Instrument panel
    (a) Instrument lighting
    (b) Charge indicator (red)

    (c) Oil pressure indicator (orange)
    (d) High beam indicator (blue)
    (e) Turn indicator light (green)
    (f) Water temperature gauge
    (g) Fuel gauge
    (h) 12-pole plug
    (k) 3-pole plug for clock
    (l) 3-pole plug for tachometer
  (m) Speedometer
    (n) Clock
    (p) Brake warning light
       with test switch

29. 12-pole round plug for instrument panel
    (seen from cable side)
30. Back-up light switch
31. Switch for warning flasher unit
32. Warning flasher sensor
33. Door switch, RH
34. Interior light
35. Door switch, LH
36. Fuel gauge sensor
37. Rear lights, RH
    A. Back-up light
    B. Rear light
    C. Turn indicator
    D. Stop light
38. Rear lights, LH
    A. Back-up light
    B. Rear light
    C. Turn indicator
    D. Stop light
39. License plate light
40. Warning buzzer
41. Warning buzzer contact
 X Flat pin connector

Cable coding:

Firing order: 1 - 3 - 4 - 2

1.5 GN — BL

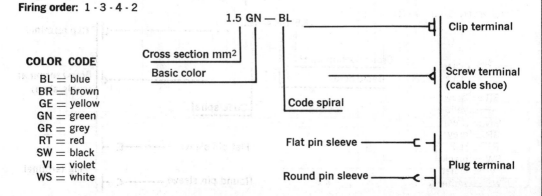

COLOR CODE

BL = blue
BR = brown
GE = yellow
GN = green
GR = grey
RT = red
SW = black
VI = violet
WS = white

Cross section mm^2

Basic color

Code spiral

Clip terminal

Screw terminal
(cable shoe)

Flat pin sleeve

Round pin sleeve

Plug terminal

KEY TO
WIRING DIAGRAM — 2002 (Manual Transmission)
(See Pages 128-129)

 1. Turn indicator, front RH with parking light
 2. Headlight, RH
 4. Headlight, LH
 5. Turn indicator, LH with parking light
 6. Alternator
 7. Regulator
 8. Distributor
 9. Starter
10. Battery
11. Stop light switch
12. Ignition coil
13. Oil pressure switch
14. Remote thermometer sensor
15. Fuse box
16. Windshield washer pump
17. Windshield wiper motor
18. Delay relay
19. Heater blower
20. Ignition/starter switch
    Switch positions:
    I   Stop
    II   Garage
    III Drive
    IV   Start
21. Light switch
22. Cigarette lighter
23. Windshield wiper switch
24. Heater switch
25. Turn indicator/windshield washer switch
26. Dimmer with flasher unit
27. Horn ring
28. Instrument panel
    (a) Instrument lighting
    (b) Charge indicator (red)
    (c) Oil pressure indicator (orange)
    (d) High beam indicator (blue)

 (e) Turn indicator light (green)
 (f) Water temperature gauge
 (g) Fuel gauge
 (h) 12-pole plug
 (k) 3-pole plug for clock
 (l) 3-pole plug for tachometer
 (m) Speedometer
 (n) Clock
 (p) Brake warning light
     with test switch
29. 12-pole round plug for instrument panel
    (seen from cable side)
30. Back-up light switch
31. Switch for warning flasher unit
32. Warning flasher sensor
33. Door switch, RH
34. Interior light
35. Door switch, LH
36. Fuel gauge sensor
37. Rear lights, RH
    A. Back-up light
    B. Rear light
    C. Turn indicator
    D. Stop light
38. Rear lights, LH
    A. Back-up light
    B. Rear light
    C. Turn indicator
    D. Stop light
39. License plate light
40. Horn, RH
41. Horn, LH
42. Horn relay
43. Warning buzzer
44. Warning buzzer contact
 X Flat pin connector

Firing order: 1 - 3 - 4 - 2

COLOR CODE

    BL = blue
    BR = brown
    GE = yellow
    GN = green
    GR = grey
    RT = red
    SW = black
    VI = violet
    WS = white

Cable coding:

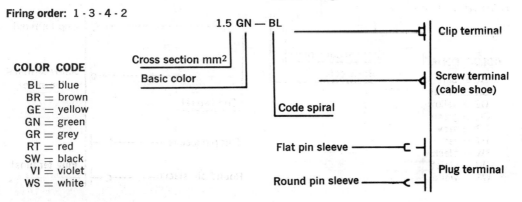

1.5 GN — BL

Cross section mm^2

Basic color

Code spiral

Clip terminal

Screw terminal
(cable shoe)

Flat pin sleeve

Round pin sleeve

Plug terminal

WIRING DIAGRAM — 2002 (Manual Transmission)

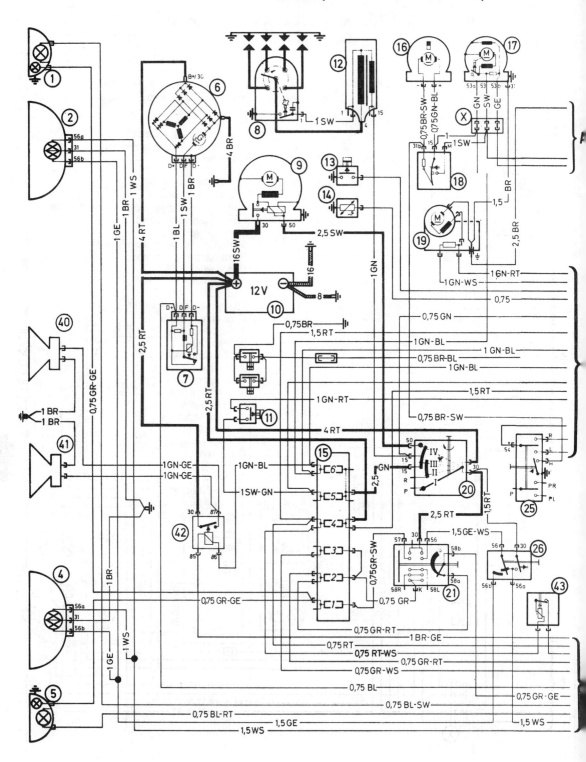

See Key on Page 127

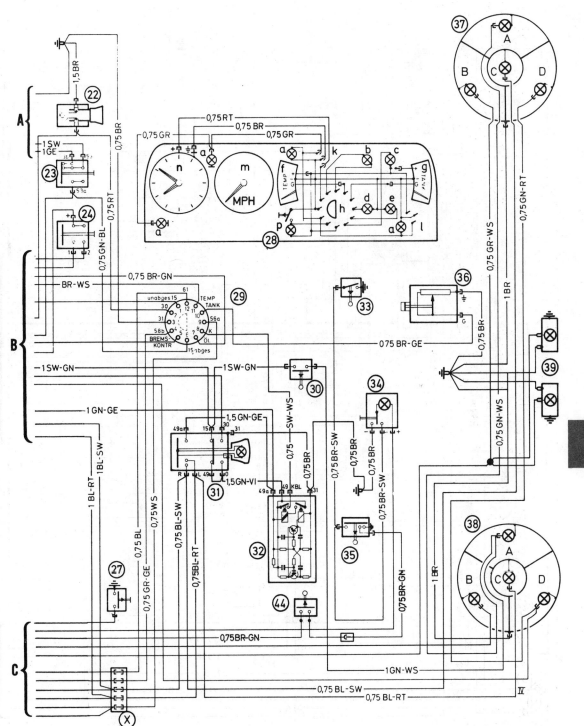

WIRING DIAGRAM — 2002 (Automatic Transmission)

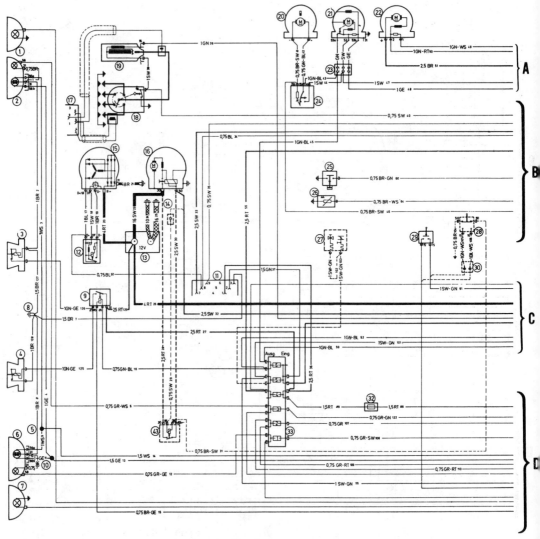

Firing order: 1 - 3 - 4 - 2

COLOR CODE

BL = blue
BR = brown
GE = yellow
GN = green
GR = grey
RT = red
SW = black
VI = violet
WS = white

See Key on Page 132

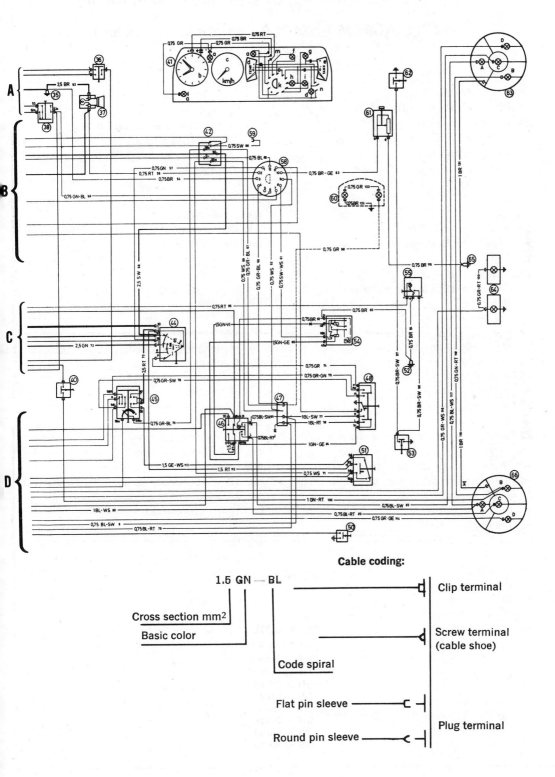

Cable coding:

1.5 GN — BL

Cross section mm² ————— Clip terminal

Basic color

Code spiral ————— Screw terminal (cable shoe)

Flat pin sleeve ————

Round pin sleeve ————— Plug terminal

KEY TO
WIRING DIAGRAM — 2002 (Automatic Transmission)
(See Pages 130-131)

1. Turn indicator, front RH
2. Headlight, RH with parking light
3. Horn, RH
4. Horn, LH
5. Soldering point (56a)
6. Headlight, LH with parking light
7. Turn indicator, front LH
8. Ground
9. Horn relay
10. Soldering point (56b)
11. Connection for diagnosis instrument
12. Regulator
13. Battery
14. Plug connection for starter relay
15. Generator
16. Starter
17. Connection for diagnosis instrument
    with line and sensor
18. Distributor
19. Ignition coil
20. Windshield washer pump
21. Windshield wiper motor
22. Blower motor
23. 3-pole plug connection for wiper motor
24. Delay relay
25. Oil pressure switch
26. Remote thermometer sensor
27. Auto choke carburetor
28. Back-up light switch with starter lock
29. Back-up light switch
30. 2-pole plug connection
32. Flying fuse
33. Fuse box
35. Ground
36. Blower switch
37. Cigarette lighter
38. Wiper switch
40. Stop light switch
41. Instrument panel
    (a) Instrument lighting
    (b) Clock
    (c) Speedometer
    (d) Cooling water temperature gauge

    (e) Fuel gauge
    (f) Charge indicator (red)
    (g) Oil pressure indicator (orange)
    (h) High beam (blue)
    (l) Turn indicator light (green)
    (k) 12-pole plug
    (m) 3-pole plug (clock)
    (n) Tachometer
42. 5-pole plug
43. Starter relay
44. Ignition/starter switch
    Switch positions:
    I   Stop
    II 0
    III Drive
    IV Start
45. Light switch
46. Warning flasher switch
47. 4-pole plug
48. Turn indicator switch
50. Horn button
51. Dimmer switch
52. Ground
53. Door switch, LH
54. Warning flasher sensor
55. Interior light
58. 12-pole connector for instrument panel
59. Connector for tachometer
60. Transmission quadrant lighting
61. Fuel gauge sensor
62. Door switch, RH
63. Rear lights, RH
    A. Back-up light
    B. Stop light
    C. Turn indicator
    D. Rear light
64. Number plate light
65. Ground
66. Rear lights, LH
    A. Back-up light
    B. Stop light
    C. Turn indicator
    D. Rear light

KEY TO
WIRING DIAGRAM — 2002ti
(See Pages 134-135)

1. Turn indicator, front RH
2. Headlight, RH with parking light
3. Horn, RH
4. Horn, LH
5. Headlight, LH with parking light
6. Turn indicator, front LH
7. Alternator
8. Regulator
9. Horn relay
10. Distributor
11. Starter
12. Battery
13. Stop light switch
14. Ignition coil
15. Oil pressure switch
16. Remote thermometer sensor
17. Fuse box
18. Windshield washer pump
19. Windshield wiper motor
20. Delay relay
21. Heater blower
22. Ignition/starter switch
    Switch positions:
    I   Stop
    II Garage
    III Drive
    IV Start
23. Light switch
24. Cigarette lighter
25. Windshield wiper switch
26. Blower switch
27. Turn indicator/parking light/
    windshield washer switch
28. Dimmer switch with flasher unit
29. Horn ring

30. Instrument panel
    (a) Instrument lighting
    (b) Charge indicator (red)
    (c) Oil pressure indicator (orange)
    (d) High beam indicator (blue)
    (e) Turn indicator light (green)
    (f) Water temperature gauge
    (g) Fuel gauge
    (h) 12-pole plug
    (k) 3-pole plug for clock
    (l) 3-pole plug for tachometer
    (m) Speedometer
    (n) Clock
    (p) Tachometer
31. 12-pole round plug for instrument
    panel (seen from cable side)
32. Back-up light switch
33. Flasher unit
34. Cable for heated rear window
    (special equipment)
35. Door switch, RH
36. Interior light
37. Door switch, LH
38. Fuel gauge sensor
39. Rear lights, RH
    A. Back-up light
    B. Rear light
    C. Turn indicator
    D. Stop light
40. Rear lights, RH
    A. Back-up light
    B. Rear light
    C. Turn indicator
    D. Stop light
41. License plate light
X   Flat pin connector

Cable coding:

Firing order: 1 - 3 - 4 - 2

COLOR CODE

BL = blue
BR = brown
GE = yellow
GN = green
GR = grey
RT = red
SW = black
VI = violet
WS = white

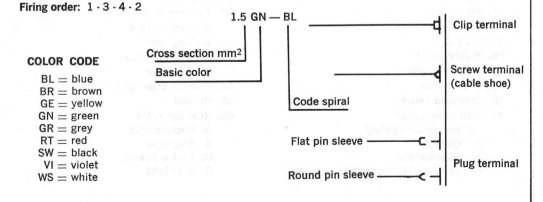

1.5 GN — BL

Cross section mm^2

Basic color

Code spiral

Clip terminal

Screw terminal
(cable shoe)

Flat pin sleeve

Round pin sleeve

Plug terminal

9

WIRING DIAGRAM — 2002ti

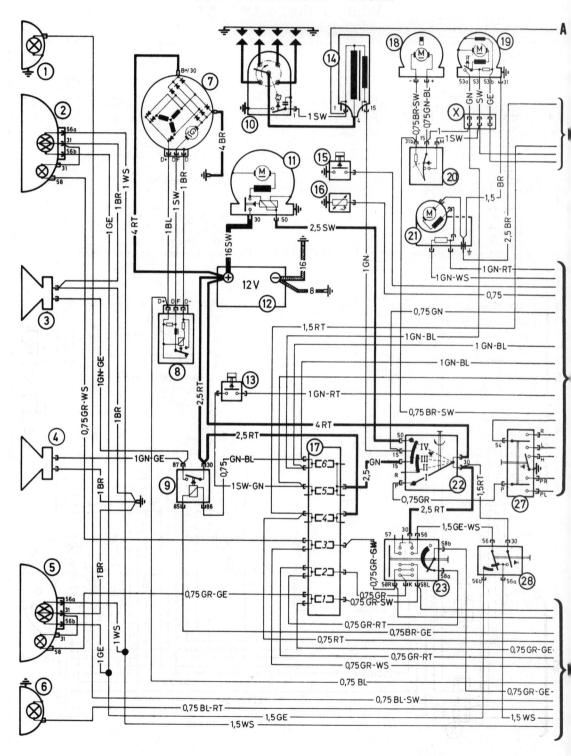

See Key on Page 133

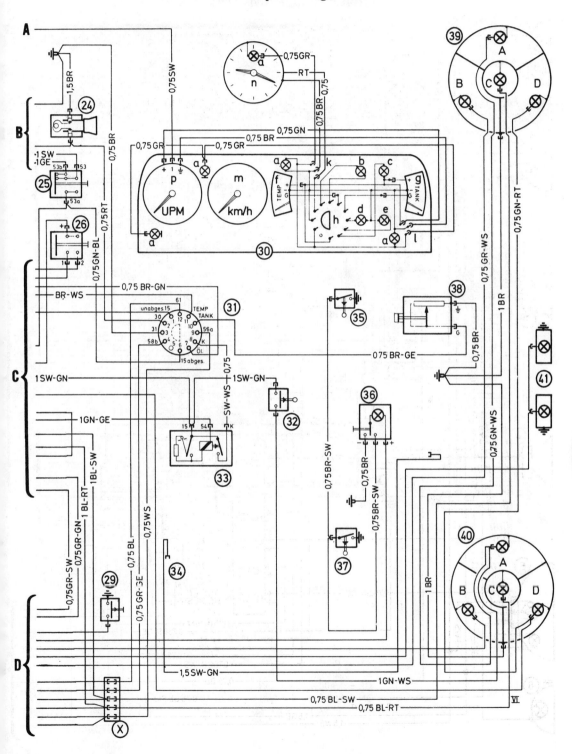

WIRING DIAGRAM — 2002tii

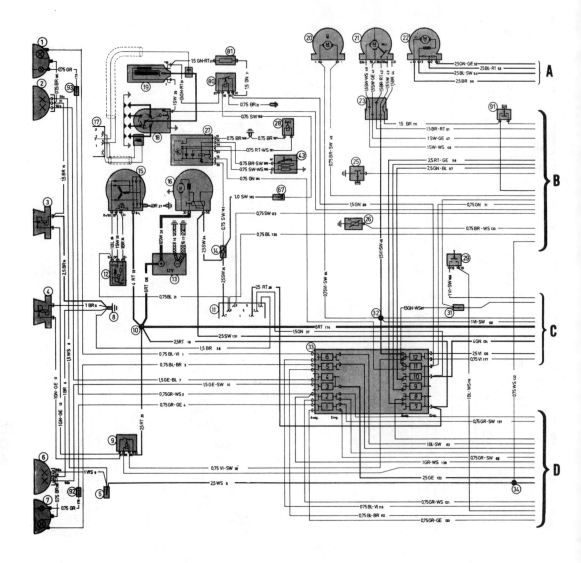

Firing order: 1 - 3 - 4 - 2

COLOR CODE

BL = blue	RT = red
BR = brown	SW = black
GE = yellow	VI = violet
GN = green	WS = white
GR = grey	

See Key on Page 138

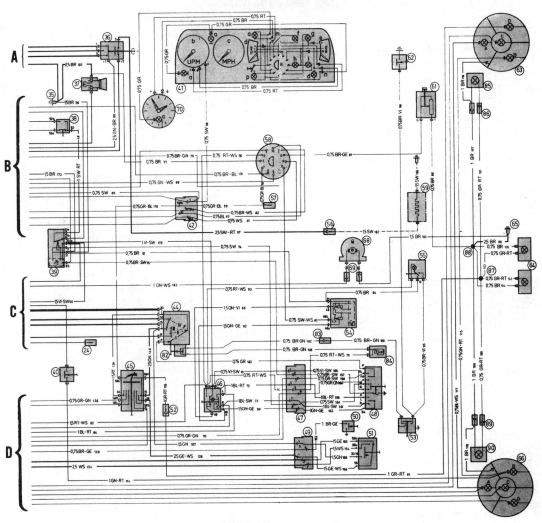

Cable coding:

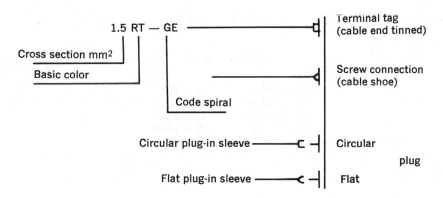

1.5 RT — GE

Cross section mm²

Basic color

Code spiral

Circular plug-in sleeve

Flat plug-in sleeve

Terminal tag (cable end tinned)

Screw connection (cable shoe)

Circular

plug

Flat

KEY TO

WIRING DIAGRAM — 2002tii

(See Pages 136-137)

1. Turn signal with parking light, RF
2. Headlight, right
3. Horn, right
4. Horn, left
5. Connection for fog light relay
6. Headlight, left
7. Turn signal with parking light, LF
8. Ground
9. Horn relay
10. Soldered joint
11. Connection for diagnostic device
12. Regulator
13. Battery
14. Connection for injection system
15. Alternator
16. Starter
17. Connection for diagnostic device
18. Distributor
19. Coil
20. Windshield washer pump
21. Windshield wiper motor
22. Ventilation motor
23. Plug connector
24. Connection for radio
25. Oil pressure switch
26. Coolant thermometer contact
27. Time switch
28. Starter valve
29. Switch for back-up light
31. Connection for fuel pump
32. Soldering point
33. Fuse box
34. Soldering point
35. Ground
36. Fan switch
37. Lighter
38. Wiper speed switch
39. Wipe-wash-contact
40. Stop light switch
41. Instrument panel
    (a) Panel light
    (b) Tachometer
    (c) Speedometer
    (d) Coolant temperature indicator
    (e) Fuel gauge
    (f) Battery charge light (red)
    (g) Oil pressure control (orange)
    (h) High beam headlight control (blue)
    (i) Turn indicator control (green)
    (k) Plug connector 12-phase
    (m) Plug connector 3-phase (clock)
    (n) Plug connector 3-phase (tachometer)
    (p) Brake fluid control (red)
42. Plug connector 5-phase
43. Temperature-time switch

44. Ignition starter switch
    I   = stop
    II = 0
    III = drive
    IV = start
45. Light switch
46. Hazard warning flasher switch
47. Plug contact 9-phase for dir. switch
48. Driving direction switch
49. Plug contact 6-phase for low beam headlight
50. Horn button
51. Low beam headlight switch
52. Connection for license plate light and fog light
53. Door double contact
54. Hazard warning flasher contact
55. Interior light
56. Connector for heated rear window
57. Connector for stick shift cluster
58. Connector 12-phased to instruments board
59. Heated rear window
60. Cluster
61. Fuel indicator contact
62. Door contact
63. Rear light, right
    A. Back-up light
    B. Stop light
    C. Turn indicator
    D. Taillight
64. License plate light
65. Ground
66. Taillight, left
    A. Back-up light
    B. Stop light
    C. Turn indicator
    D. Taillight
67. Connection for power ignition system
68. Fuel pump
69. Plug connection to fuel pump
70. Clock
80. Relay for power ignition system
81. Pre-resistor
82. Hazard warning buzzer contact
83. Connection for hazard warning buzzer
84. Hazard warning buzzer
85. Lateral position light, right
86. Connection for lateral position light
87. Soldering point 58 k
88. Soldering point 31
89. Connection for lateral position light, left
90. Lateral position light, left
91. Brake fluid control switch
92. Line connector
93. Line connector

WIRING DIAGRAM — 2002-2002A LATE MODELS
(See Key on Page 142)

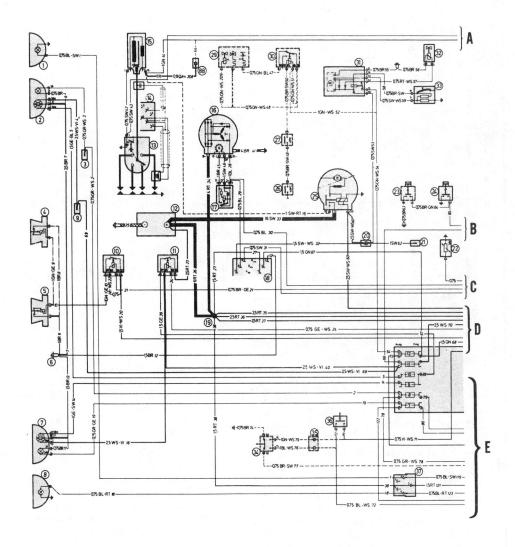

WIRING DIAGRAM — 2002-2002A LATE MODELS

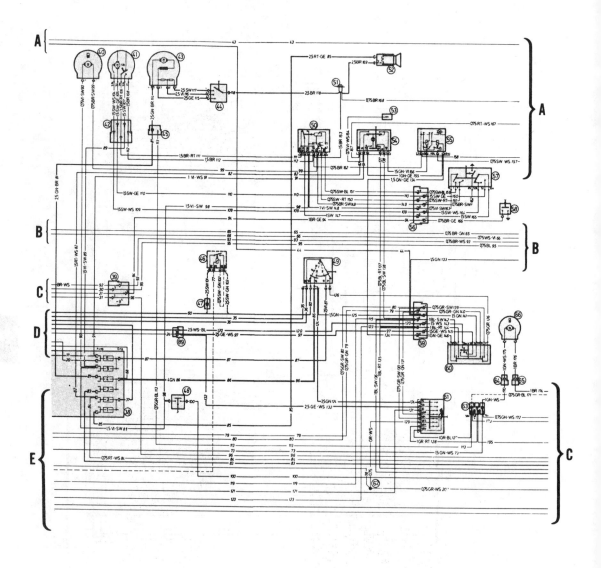

See Key on Page 142

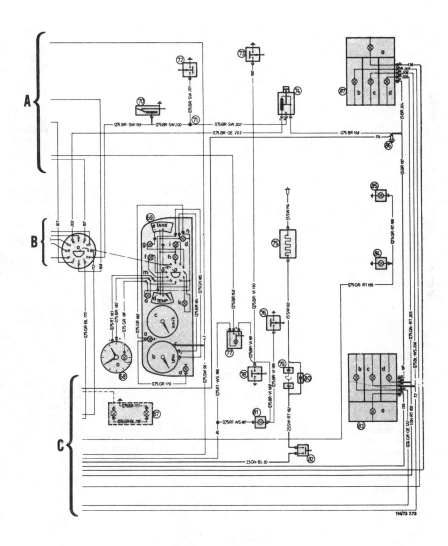

KEY TO
WIRING DIAGRAM — 2002-2002A LATE MODELS
(See Pages 139-141)

1. Turn indicator, front right
2. Headlight, right, with parking light
3. Connection for headlight wiper unit
4. Horn, right (optional)
5. Horn, left
6. Ground
7. Headlight, left, with parking light
8. Turn indicator, front left
9. Connection for fog lamp and extra headlight relay
10. Horn relay
11. Dipped beam relay
12. Battery, 12V
13. Distributor
14. Connection for diagnosis unit with cable and transducer
15. Coil
16. Alternator
17. Voltage regulator
18. Connection for diagnosis unit
19. Solder tag 30
20. 1-pole plug
21. Connection 50
22. Remote thermometer sensor
23. Brake fluid telltale (optional)
24. Oil pressure sensor
25. Starter
26. Water temperature sensor (only on automatic)
27. Air temperature sensor (only on automatic)
29. Automatic choke (only on automatic)
30. Switch-over relay
31. Time relay (on tii only)
32. Starting valve (on tii only)
33. Temperature/time switch (on tii only)
34. Relay for reversing lights with starting lock (only on automatic)
35. 2-pole plug (only on automatic)
36. Relay for reversing lights
37. 5-pole plug
38. Fuse box
39. 5-pole plug
40. Screenwasher plug
41. Wiper motor
42. 5-pole plug for wiper motor
43. Blower motor
44. Blower switch
45. 2-pole plug for blower motor
46. Starter relay (only on automatic)

47. 1-pole plug
48. Stoplight switch
49. Ignition/starter switch
50. Intermittent wipe control unit
51. Ground
52. Cigarette lighter
53. Connection for radio
54. Hazard warning flasher switch
55. Hazard warning flasher unit
56. Plug for wiper switch
57. Wiper circuit (intermittent wipe unit, optional)
58. Horn contact
59. Plug for turn indicator and low beam switch
60. Turn indicator and dipped beam switch
61. Light switch
62. Solder tag 58 S
63. 3-pole connection
64. 1-pole plug to fuel pump
65. 1-pole plug to fuel pump
66. Fuel pump
67. Automatic transmission panel lighting

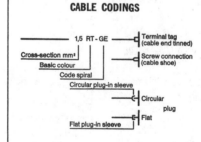

CABLE CODINGS

1,5 RT - GE — Terminal tag (cable end tinned)
Cross-section mm² — Screw connection (cable shoe)
Basic colour
Code spiral
Circular plug-in sleeve — Circular plug
Flat plug-in sleeve — Flat plug

COLOR CODE

BL = blue		RT = red
BR = brown		SW = black
GE = yellow		VI = violet
GR = grey		WS = white
GN = green		

68. Clock (on tii only)
69. Combination instrument
   a. Dial illumination
   b. Revolution counter (only on tii and as optional extra, otherwise clock)
   c. Speedometer
   d. Coolant thermometer
   e. Fuel gauge
   f. Battery charge indicator (red)
   g. Oil pressure indicator (red)
   h. Headlight main beam indicator (blue)
   i. Turn indicator (green)
   k. Central indicator (choke, handbrake, fuel reserve)
   m. 3-pole socket (clock)
   n. 3-pole socket (revolution counter)
   o. 12-pole socket
70. Choke (except on tii)
71. Solder tag
72. Handbrake switch
73. Door operated switch, right
74. Fuel gauge float
75. Heated rear window
76. Rear door contact (only on touring)
77. Interior light
78. Door operated switch, left
79. Contact plate, left (only on touring)
80. 1-pole plug for heated rear window
81. Luggage compartment light (only on touring)
82. Switch for heated rear window
83. Rear light cluster left
   a. Turn indicator
   b. Rear light
   c. Backup light
   d. Stoplight
84. License plate light, left
85. License plate light, right
86. Ground
87. Rear light cluster
   a. Turn indicator
   b. Rear light
   c. Backup light
   d. Stoplight
88. Resistance cable for high-performance ignition system (only on Turbo and with high-performance ignition system as optional extra)
89. 2-pole plug

CHAPTER TEN

CLUTCH, TRANSMISSION
AND DRIVE SHAFT

This chapter covers the clutch master cylinder, slave cylinder, clutch assembly, 4-speed manual transmission, and drive shaft. Detailed instructions for the automatic transmission are not given, but checks and adjustments to the automatic transmission are given as appropriate for the average home mechanic. Overhaul or major service to automatic transmission should be referred to your BMW dealer or transmission specialist. Instructions are given for removal of the automatic transmission.

Special tools are needed in many cases to work on the manual transmission. The illustrations show the special tools in actual use. However, a well-equipped mechanic may be able to substitute or fabricate equivalent tools as required. For the average mechanic, it may be quicker and cheaper to refer repair to a transmission specialist after removal of the defective unit from the car.

CLUTCH MASTER CYLINDER/
SLAVE CYLINDER

The clutch master cylinder and hydraulic slave cylinder work together to assist in the shifting of gears. Preventive periodic maintenance is not required, but the slave cylinder and master cylinder should be inspected periodically for signs of oil leaks. The master cylinder reser-

voir should be checked frequently and replenished as necessary. **Figure 1** shows the oil reservoir, master cylinder, slave cylinder, and associated hoses. The slave cylinder is attached to the clutch operating lever to help disengage the clutch release bearing.

Bleeding Clutch Hydraulic System

1. Fill up the reservoir with clean fluid.

2. Connect a bleed tube and container to the slave cylinder bleed screw, as shown in **Figure 2**.

3. Open bleed screw on slave cylinder and watch fluid running through bleed hose. When no bubbles are seen in the bleed hose, close the bleed screw. Do not permit the level of fluid in the reservoir to drop below the supply line level. Replenish frequently or continuously by having an assistant replenish the reservoir as it is being drained.

Adjusting Clutch Play

Clutch adjustment is made at the clutch release lever in the clutch bell housing.

1. Loosen locknut, as shown in **Figure 3**.

2. Adjust the adjustment nut until the clutch release lever travel is 0.12-0.14 in. (3.0-3.5mm) before engagement of the throwout bearing

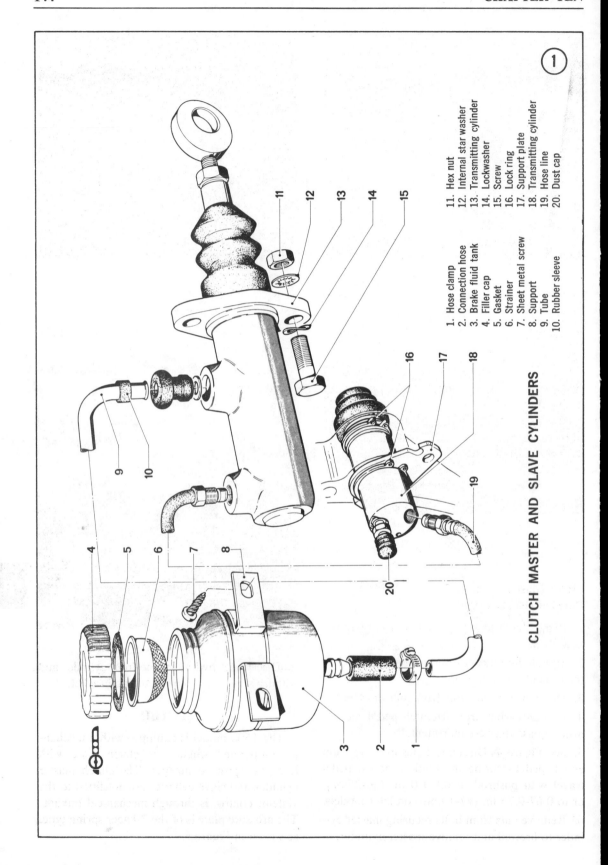

CLUTCH MASTER AND SLAVE CYLINDERS

1. Hose clamp
2. Connection hose
3. Brake fluid tank
4. Filler cap
5. Gasket
6. Strainer
7. Sheet metal screw
8. Support
9. Tube
10. Rubber sleeve
11. Hex nut
12. Internal star washer
13. Transmitting cylinder
14. Lockwasher
15. Screw
16. Lock ring
17. Support plate
18. Transmitting cylinder
19. Hose line
20. Dust cap

(release bearing) against the clutch pressure plate.

Clutch Master Cylinder
Removal/Replacement

1. Bleed clutch hydraulic system, as previously described.

2. Siphon fluid out of reservoir until it is below the level of the supply line union.

3. Disconnect supply line from master cylinder.

4. Loosen carpet around clutch pedal mechanism in passenger compartment.

5. See **Figure 4**. Disconnect pushrod (1) from clutch pedal. During installation, adjust pedal travel with pushrod to 0.8-1.0 in. (20-25mm) or to 0.67-0.75 in. (17-19mm) on later models.

6. Remove nuts from bolts securing master cylinder to firewall and remove master cylinder.

Clutch Slave Cylinder
Removal/Replacement

1. Bleed clutch hydraulic system and syphon fluid out of reservoir.

2. See **Figure 5**. Remove retaining ring (1) and circlip (2).

3. Disconnect hydraulic line from cylinder and withdraw cylinder from mounting bracket.

CLUTCH

The 1600 model is equipped with a mechanically-operated single, dry clutch plate with torsional spring dampener. The clutch master cylinder and slave cylinder are not fitted to the system; control is through mechanical linkage. The pressure plate is of the 3-finger spring type, as shown in **Figure 6**.

10

The 2002 models are equipped with a hydraulically-controlled single, dry clutch plate with torsional spring dampener and automatic wear adjustment. The pressure plate is of the diaphragm spring type, as shown in **Figure 7**.

Service and repair of the clutch requires removal of the transmission from the car. After removal, the clutch parts and release bearing can be serviced. Cleanliness is essential in the handling of clutch parts, as grease, oil, or dirt on the friction surfaces will cause the clutch to slip.

Removal/Installation

1. Remove transmission from car as described later in this chapter.

2. Mark the cover, pressure plate, and release lever for replacement in the same relative location.

3. Lock the flywheel so that it cannot rotate.

4. Progressively, using a diagonal pattern, loosen and remove bolts holding clutch assembly to flywheel.

5. Remove pressure plate and clutch plate from flywheel.

6. To install, reverse the above steps. The clutch plate must be centered with a centering tool, such as that shown in **Figure 8**, so that the transmission main shaft splines will engage correctly.

7. Torque tighten the pressure plate mounting bolts to 12.3 ft.-lb.

8. Lightly lubricate transmission main shaft splines before insertion into clutch plate.

Servicing

1. Thoroughly clean all parts, except for the clutch plate, in a suitable solvent.

2. Check all parts carefully for wear, cracks, and other defects.

3. Check the clutch plate for oil-soaked or cracked facings, warping, loose rivets, excessive wear, and broken springs. Repair is by replacement.

4. If the clutch plate appears in good condition, use a dial gauge to check the runout of the plate. Maximum permissible runout is 0.024 in. (0.6mm).

5. Check the friction surface of the pressure plate for scoring, burn marks (blue tinted areas), and cracks. If defective or badly worn, replace with new unit. Minor imperfections can be removed with fine glass cloth, or equivalent. The finished surface should have a mirror-like finish.

6. Check condition of the flywheel for scoring and burn marks. If defective, remove as described in Chapter Five and service or replace, as required.

7. Check condition of the pressure plate fingers or diaphragm spring for wear and damage. Repair is by replacement.

8. Check condition of pressure plate springs. If broken, replace with new unit.

RELEASE BEARING

Removal/Servicing

1. Disconnect mechanical linkage or slave cylinder linkage from release lever. See **Figure 9** on the following page.

2. Remove transmission, as discussed later in this chapter.

3. See **Figure 10**. Unhook spring ends from release lever. During installation, the angle seal (1) must be between ball pin and release lever.

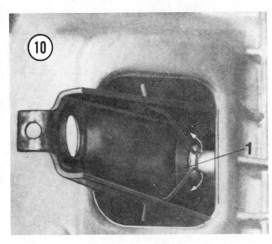

4. Remove release lever and release bearing from bell housing and transmission main shaft by pulling off towards the front of the bell housing.

5. Detach release lever from retainer springs, as shown in **Figure 11**.

6. Inspect all parts for wear and damage. The release bearing is permanently lubricated and sealed. If the release bearing shows signs of lubricant leakage, replace with new one. If the

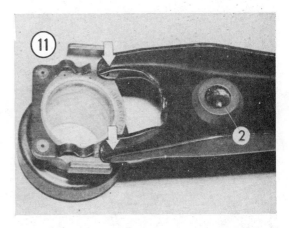

gasket (2) in the release lever is damaged, replace with new one.

7. To install, reverse above steps. Coat retainer springs, angle seal, and ball pin with lubricant.

8. Adjust release lever and/or clutch pedal as required.

TRANSMISSION

Removal/Installation

> **WARNING**
> *Never get under a car that is supported by a jack only. If a hoist or jackstands are not available, use sturdy wooden blocks.*

1. Raise the car on a hoist or jack it up and insert jackstands. The transmission is removed from under the car and considerable room is needed.

2. See **Figure 12**. Loosen and remove upper transmission fixing bolts.

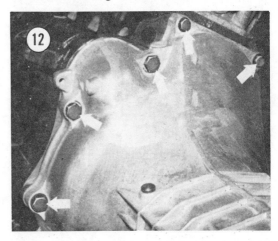

10

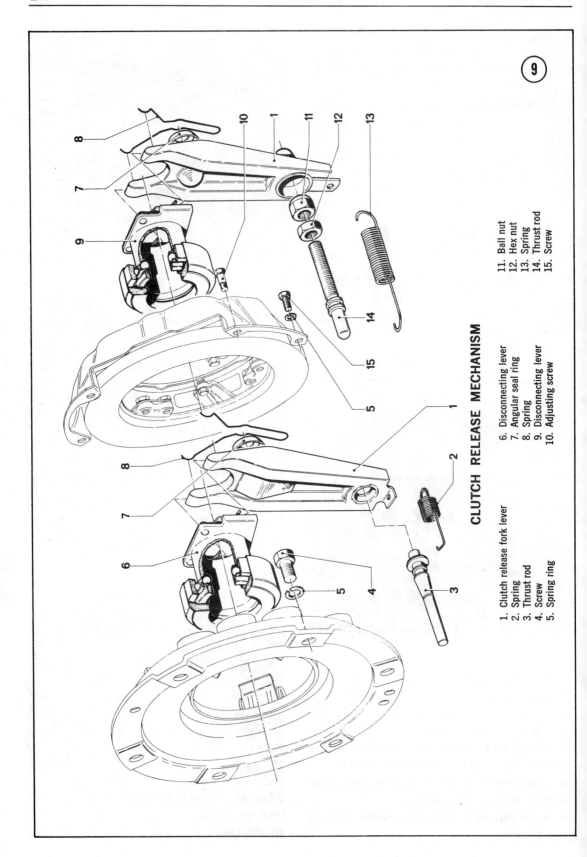

⑨

CLUTCH RELEASE MECHANISM

1. Clutch release fork lever
2. Spring
3. Thrust rod
4. Screw
5. Spring ring
6. Disconnecting lever
7. Angular seal ring
8. Spring
9. Disconnecting lever
10. Adjusting screw
11. Ball nut
12. Hex nut
13. Spring
14. Thrust rod
15. Screw

3. From inside car, lift up on gearshift boot and foam rubber ring. Remove circlip from around gearshift ball, as shown in **Figure 13**.

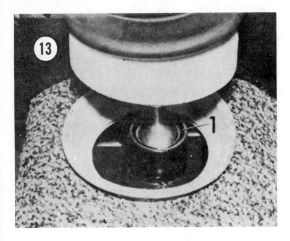

4. From under the car, remove exhaust bracket by unscrewing and removing bolts shown in **Figure 14**.

5. Disconnect the exhaust pipe from the exhaust manifold.

6. Disconnect and remove drive shaft, as discussed later in this chapter.

7. See **Figure 15**. Loosen set screw (2) and drive out bearing pin (1) from gearshift linkage.

8. Disconnect clutch release lever from slave cylinder or mechanical linkage.

9. See **Figure 16**. Loosen and remove bolts and cover plate.

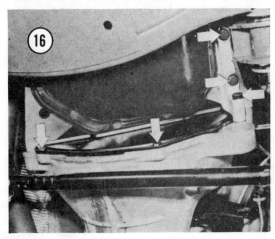

10. Support the engine with a suitable block placed between the oil sump and the front axle sub-frame.

11. At the rear of the transmission, slacken bolt (1) and pull out speedometer shaft. See **Figure 17**. Pull off connectors (2) from reverse light switch.

12. Place hydraulic jack under transmission and jack up until weight of transmission is supported.

13. Turn steering to full right-hand lock.

14. Unscrew remaining transmission fixing bolts.

15. Pull the transmission backwards until the main shaft splines are clear of the pressure plate. When clear, lower jack and pull transmission out from under car.

16. To install, reverse the above steps. Torque

10

tighten transmission to 18.1 ft.-lb. (small bolts) and 34.0 ft.-lb. (large bolts).

Disassembly/Assembly

Figures 18, 19, and 20 are exploded diagrams that provide details of the transmission and associated components.

1. Remove transmission from car and install on holding stand or suitable workbench. Remove drain plug and drain oil into suitable container.

2. See **Figure 21**. Unscrew nuts and bolts and remove bracket and stay.

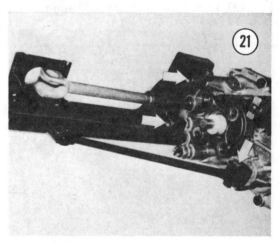

3. See **Figure 22**. Push back spring sleeve (1) and drive out pin (2). Pull out selector shaft and joint.

4. Unscrew bolts and remove exhaust support bracket.

5. See **Figure 23**. Remove release bearing and release lever, as previously described. Unscrew

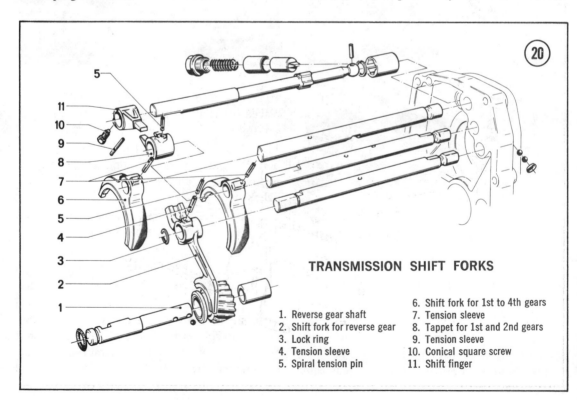

TRANSMISSION SHIFT FORKS

1. Reverse gear shaft
2. Shift fork for reverse gear
3. Lock ring
4. Tension sleeve
5. Spiral tension pin
6. Shift fork for 1st to 4th gears
7. Tension sleeve
8. Tappet for 1st and 2nd gears
9. Tension sleeve
10. Conical square screw
11. Shift finger

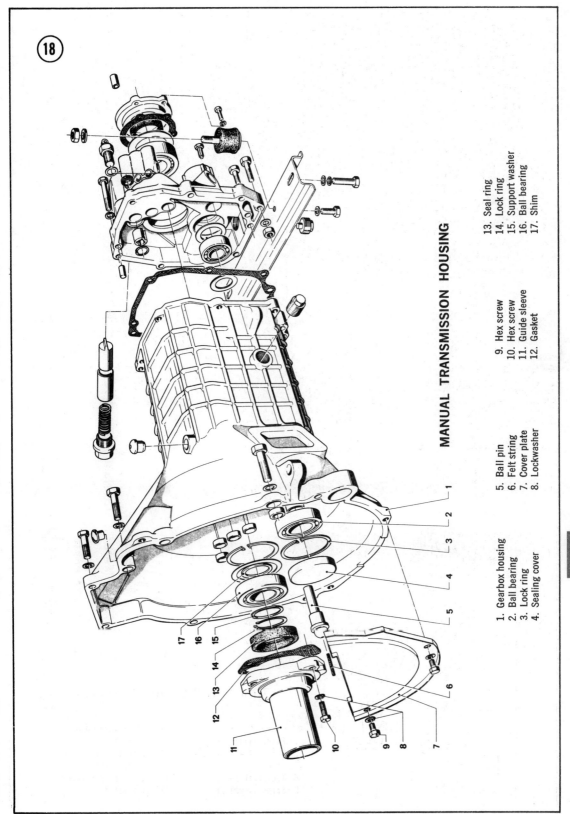

(18)

MANUAL TRANSMISSION HOUSING

1. Gearbox housing
2. Ball bearing
3. Lock ring
4. Sealing cover

5. Ball pin
6. Felt string
7. Cover plate
8. Lockwasher

9. Hex screw
10. Hex screw
11. Guide sleeve
12. Gasket

13. Seal ring
14. Lock ring
15. Support washer
16. Ball bearing
17. Shim

10

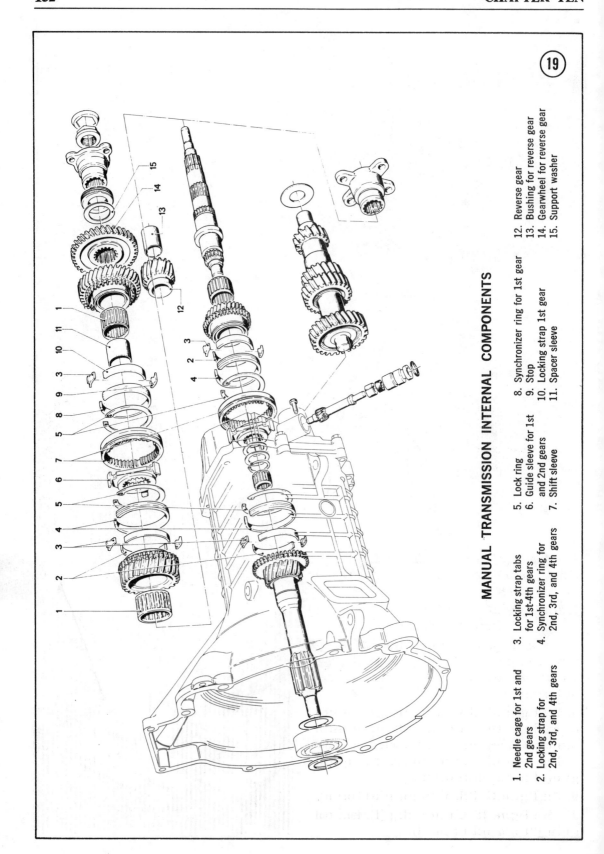

MANUAL TRANSMISSION INTERNAL COMPONENTS

1. Needle cage for 1st and 2nd gears
2. Locking strap for 2nd, 3rd, and 4th gears
3. Locking strap tabs for 1st-4th gears
4. Synchronizer ring for 2nd, 3rd, and 4th gears
5. Lock ring
6. Guide sleeve for 1st and 2nd gears
7. Shift sleeve
8. Synchronizer ring for 1st gear
9. Stop
10. Locking strap 1st gear
11. Spacer sleeve
12. Reverse gear
13. Bushing for reverse gear
14. Gearwheel for reverse gear
15. Support washer

11. Set selector rod (1) to 4th gear position and turn guide sleeve until locating pin (2) can be driven out with a punch. See **Figure 29**. Pull selector rod out forwards and remove ball bearings.

fixing bolts and remove guide sleeve and associated shims. When installing, make certain to use new gasket.

6. See **Figure 24**. Use snap ring pliers to remove circlip (1). Remove shims (2) from shaft.

7. Use a puller, as shown in **Figure 25**, to remove grooved bearing from housing. Remove shims from in back of bearing and mark for later replacement.

8. See **Figure 26**. Unscrew transmission housing cover fixing bolts and separate transmission housing after heating up the housing around the sealing cover with a torch so that the layshaft grooved bearing slides out easily.

9. See **Figure 27**. Pull off transmission housing.

10. See **Figure 28**. Unscrew plug (1), take out spring (2), and locking pin (3).

10

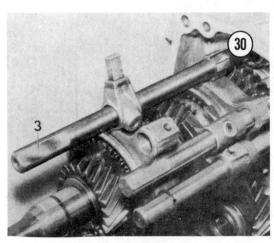

14. See **Figure 31**. Push selector rod (5) into 2nd gear position. Turn guide sleeve until locating pin (6) can be driven out with a punch. Pull selector rod out forwards. Remove selector fork.

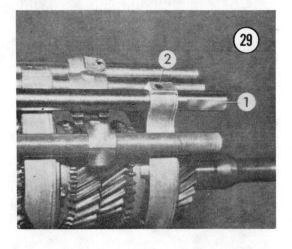

15. Push 2nd gear wheel into neutral position.

16. Unscrew set screw and remove plug-in bushing and speedometer pinion. During installation, renew O-ring and plug-in bushing if the sealing ring is defective.

17. See **Figure 32**. Pull off bumper and lift out locking plate with screwdriver. During installation, make certain the locking plate seats in the groove.

18. See **Figure 33**. Push guide sleeve (607) onto centering pin. Hold flange with tool (6039) and unscrew flange nut. Remove flange.

19. See **Figure 34**. Unscrew bolts and remove

12. See **Figure 30**. Swing selector bar upwards and withdraw selector shaft (3) forwards.

13. Set selector sleeve to neutral and remove selector fork.

support ring and shims. Mark shims for later replacement.

20. Place a 0.079 in. (2mm) metal strip between the 2nd and 3rd gears to prevent 3rd gear syn-

chromesh from being pushed off when the output shaft grooved bearing is removed. See **Figure 35**.

21. Use a puller to pull the grooved ball bearing from the output shaft and out of the housing. Remove shims and mark for later replacement. See **Figure 36**.

22. Swing drive and output shaft out to the right, as shown in **Figure 37**.

23. Drive layshaft out forward with soft hammer. Remove shims from housing and mark for later replacement.

24. Pull selector rod with selector fork and reverse idler gear out of housing cover. Remove loose ball bearings.

25. See **Figure 38**. Pull off drive shaft with needle cage (1) and selector sleeve (2) from output shaft.

10

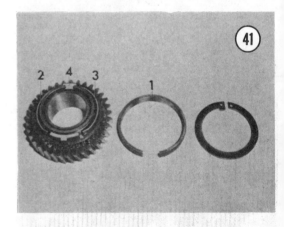

26. See **Figure 39**. Lift out circlip. Remove support disc, shim, sliding sleeve, and 3rd gear with needle cage. During installation, place the 3rd gear, guide sleeve, and thrust washer on the output shaft and install the circlip. Use a feeler gauge to measure the gap between the thrust washer and the guide sleeve and then use a shim of the proper size to reduce clearance to zero.

27. See **Figure 40**. Remove output shaft from speedometer pinion (1), thrust washer (2), reverse gear pinion (3), 1st gear pinion (4), needle cage (5), distance bushing (6), selector sleeve (7), guide sleeve (8), 2nd gear pinion (9), and needle cage (10). During installation, the ground side of the reverse gear pinion must face the 1st gear pinion.

28. Disassemble all synchromesh components, as shown in **Figure 41**. Lift out the lock ring and take off synchromesh ring (1), baulk strap (2, 3), block (4), and stop (5). Examine all parts carefully for wear and damage. If defective, replace with new parts.

29. After inspection and replacement of defective parts, assemble using reverse of above step.

NOTE: *The 1st gear synchromesh ring is color-coded with a white spot; 2nd, 3rd, and 4th have a blue spot.*

30. Push synchromesh ring into selector sleeve. Front edge of selector sleeve and synchromesh ring must be in the same plane. If the pattern of wear of the synchromesh ring is mostly at the 2 abutting ends, the synchromesh ring must be replaced with new one. After assembly, it should be possible to turn the synchromesh ring easily by hand.

31. Assemble the output shaft. See **Figure 42**. Measure dimension (A) and record. The measurement should be 5.433 ± 0.0039 in. (138 ± 0.1mm). Add proper size shim (Y) to output shaft, as shown in **Figure 43**.

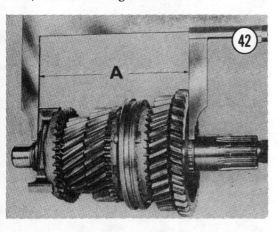

32. Measure thickness of speedometer pinion and record as dimension (B). Press speedometer pinion onto output shaft.

33. See **Figure 44**. Press grooved bearing into transmission housing cover. Measure distance (C) and record.

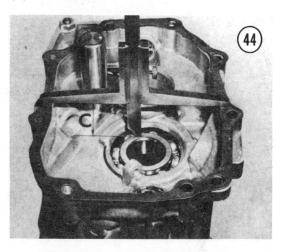

34. See **Figure 45**. A shim of the proper size should be added as given below. The shim is shown as (X).

Example: (A) Theoretical	5.433 in.	(138.0mm)
+(B)	0.583 in.	(14.8mm)
	6.016 in.	(152.8mm)
−(C)	1.457 in.	(37.0mm)
	4.559 in.	(115.8mm)
(D) Actual	4.559 in.	(115.8mm)
(D) Theoretical	4.567 in.	(116.0mm)
(X)	0.008 in.	(0.2mm)

35. Check condition of layshaft, bearing, and gears. To disassemble, pull off bearing and press off 4th gear pinion. If the gear pinions are damaged and need replacement, replace them in pairs only.

36. Remove circlip, as shown in **Figure 46**. Press off 3rd gear pinion. Smooth off any scoring on the layshaft with fine emery cloth.

37. To assemble layshaft, lightly lubricate the layshaft, heat 3rd and 4th gear pinions to 275°F and press onto layshaft. Pressure required to install is approximately 8,800 lb. Install bearing.

38. See **Figure 47**. Check distance (A) from housing sealing surface to circlip. Record the measurement.

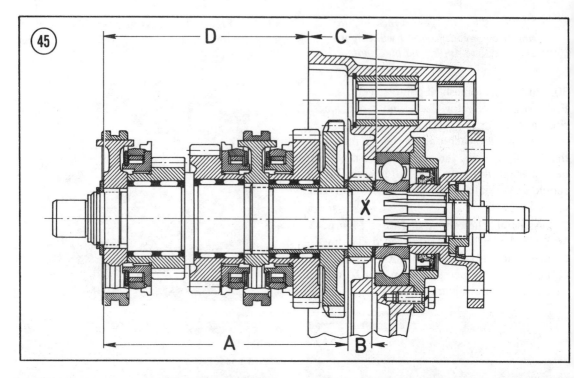

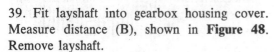

39. Fit layshaft into gearbox housing cover. Measure distance (B), shown in **Figure 48**. Remove layshaft.

40. See **Figure 49**. Determine thickness of shim (C) as follows:

Example:	(A)	6.508 in. (165.3mm)
	(B)	6.496 in. (165.0mm)
	(C)	0.012 in. (0.3mm)

41. Check condition of bushing in reverse idler pinion. If defective, press out old bushing and

press in new one. When installed, use a reamer to ream the bushing to 0.838 in. (21.3mm).

42. Check condition of selector forks. Replace if defective.

43. See **Figure 50**. Remove reverse light switch (1) and seal cap (2). Arrestor balls are installed with a screwdriver through the open holes, as discussed below.

44. Insert arrestor ball through hole, press downward, and push reverse gear selector rod with reverse idler pinion into housing cover until first arrestor ball locates.

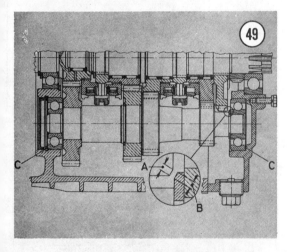

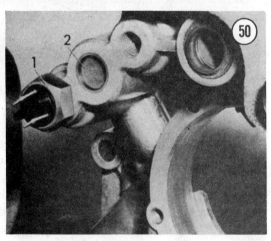

45. Place shim (C) in housing cover and press in layshaft.

46. Insert drive and output shafts into housing cover.

47. Place shim (X) in front of speedometer pinion. Drive grooved bearing into housing cover.

48. Check tooth engagement. Tooth engagement can be changed with shim (C) in front of the layshaft bearing.

49. See **Figure 51**. Measure distance (A) from housing cover to ball bearing. Measure flange height (B) of sealing cover with seal in position, as shown in **Figure 52**. Determine thickness of shim required so that there is zero play between bearing outer race and sealing cover.

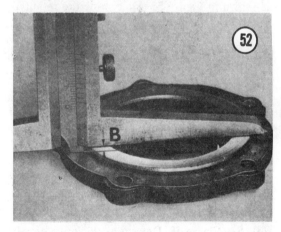

50. Install the shim and sealing cover. Secure and lock output flange.

51. Push 1st/2nd gear selector fork into selector sleeve. Insert locking and arrestor ball. Fit selector rod and secure selector fork with locating pin.

52. Push 3rd/4th gear selector fork into selector sleeve. Fit selector shaft and locking pin.

10

53. Insert locking and arrestor balls, as shown in **Figure 53**.

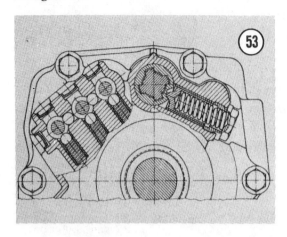

54. Fit 3rd/4th gear selector rod. Secure selector fork with locating pin.

55. Install sealing cap, reverse light switch, and speedometer pinion.

56. Install 0.039 in. (1mm) shim and grooved bearing into housing.

57. See **Figure 54**. Measure distance (A) from housing sealing surface to bearing. Dimension (B) is electrically engraved on the input shaft, as shown in **Figure 55**. Determine the required thickness of shim (X) from data in **Table 1**.

58. Place shim (X) on the input shaft. Place shim (C), which was determined for tooth engagement, on grooved bearing. Lightly coat with grease to hold it in place. See **Figure 56**.

59. Slip the gearbox housing over the gear assembly. Use a pressure device, as shown in

Table 1   SHIM SPECIFICATIONS

A mm	B	X mm
153.9	45-50	0.5
	35-40	0.6
	25-30	0.7
153.8	45-50	0.4
	35-40	0.5
	25-30	0.6
153.7	45-50	0.3
	35-40	0.4
	25-30	0.5
156.6	45-50	0.2
	35-40	0.3
	25-30	0.4

Figure 57, to press the input shaft into the ball bearing and the housing onto the housing cover. Install bolts and secure housing cover.

60. Insert circlip into groove in input shaft. Measure clearance from circlip to ball bearing to determine thickness of shim required. Remove circlip, install shim, and reinstall circlip.

61. Fit guide sleeve for clutch release collar.

62. Install drain plug and fill transmission to proper level with transmission lubricant.

63. Install transmission into car using reverse steps of removal.

64. Adjust release lever and clutch pedal travel, as required.

GEARSHIFT LEVER

Figure 58 shows the detail of the gearshift lever and associated parts. Maintenance is normally not required. However, the linkages and general fit of bushings, washers, and pins should be inspected from time to time and, if necessary, replaced. Removal of the gearshift is discussed under *Transmission Removal.*

AUTOMATIC TRANSMISSION

Maintenance and repair of the automatic transmission is complex and should be referred to your dealer or transmission specialist. The following checks and adjustments should help prevent costly repairs.

Oil Check

Check the automatic transmission oil level at least every 8,000 miles (12,500 miles on late models). Replenish with high quality automatic transmission fluid as required. Be careful not to overfill, as damage to the seals can result. To check the oil level, proceed as follows.

1. Start the engine and run it until normal operating temperature is reached.

2. Apply brakes and move the shift lever through all drive positions and place the lever in PARK.

3. With engine running, remove transmission dipstick, clean with lint-free cloth, and return it to transmission.

4. Remove stick and examine level on dipstick gauge. It should be between the low and full marks. Replenish as necessary.

5. Visually inspect the color and condition of the oil on the dipstick. Normal color of the oil is red. If the color is abnormal, drain and replace. If the oil has a varnish-like quality or is blackened, refer service to a transmission specialist.

Oil Leakage Check

Oil leakage may occur at the junction of the transmission and drive shaft, oil tube connectors, oil pressure inspection holes, and breather pipe. Abnormal oil usage usually indicates leaks that should be stopped before severe damage is done. To inspect for oil leaks, proceed as follows.

1. Raise car on hoist or jack up and install jackstands.

2. Clean outside of transmission case with cleaning solvent to remove dirt and oil accumulations.

3. Start engine and warm up.

4. Shift gear lever to DRIVE to increase oil pressure and circulation within transmission.

5. Inspect all outside surfaces for signs of leaks. Leakage of transmission oil is distinctive by its reddish color.

6. If leaks are detected, refer service and repair to transmission specialist.

Selector Lever Adjustment

1. See **Figure 59.** Check bearing bracket for tightness.

2. Place selector lever in NEUTRAL (O) position.

10

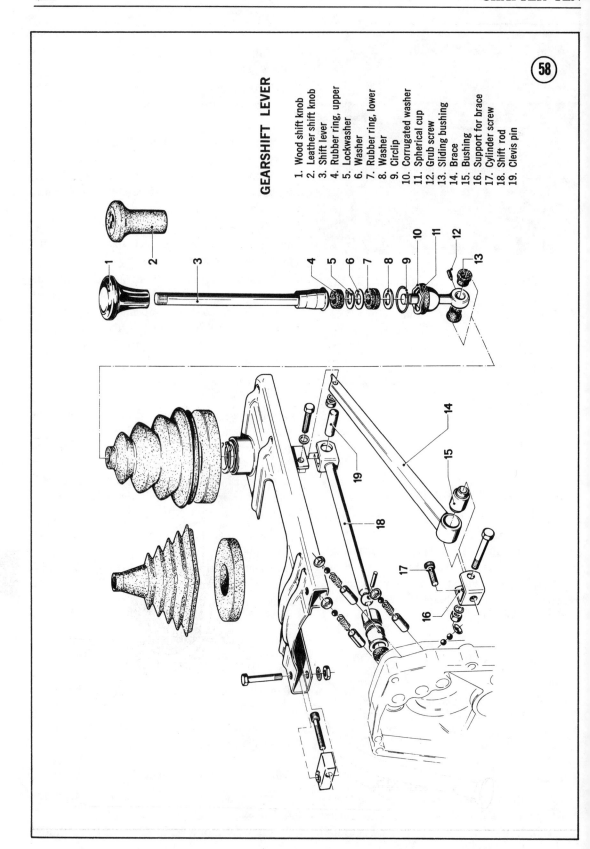

GEARSHIFT LEVER

1. Wood shift knob
2. Leather shift knob
3. Shift lever
4. Rubber ring, upper
5. Lockwasher
6. Washer
7. Rubber ring, lower
8. Washer
9. Circlip
10. Corrugated washer
11. Spherical cup
12. Grub screw
13. Sliding bushing
14. Brace
15. Bushing
16. Support for brace
17. Cylinder screw
18. Shift rod
19. Clevis pin

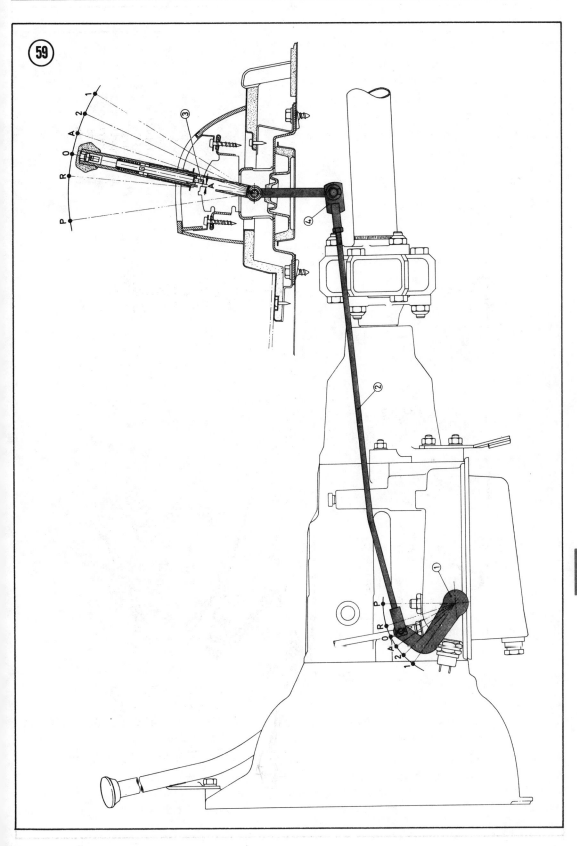

3. Disconnect selector lever (1) from selector rod (2) by removing clip and pin at linkage.

4. Adjust the length of the selector rod until the stop lug contacts the gearshift gate.

5. Shorten length of selector rod with eye-bolt (4) by 3 turns.

6. Clearance (A) between stop lug and stop must be 0.039 in. (1mm).

7. Reconnect selector lever and selector rod.

Accelerator Linkage Adjustment

1. Remove air cleaner.

2. See **Figure 60**. Remove accelerator cable. Press accelerator pedal down to the kick down stop into full acceleration position.

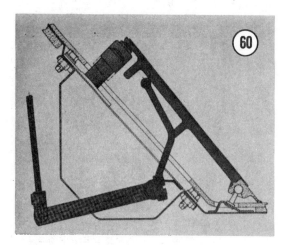

3. In this position the throttle valve must be fully open, but the throttle valve must not extend beyond the vertical position. Adjust by bending the stop.

4. Check to see that kick down stop has not lifted. Adjust the length of the accelerator linkage with the eyebolt.

Accelerator Cable Adjustment

1. See **Figure 61**. Remove accelerator cable from rotary shaft. Press down accelerator linkage to full acceleration position.

2. Determine full acceleration position by repeatedly pulling accelerator cable. The holes in the fork head must match the hole on the rotary selector so that the pin can be inserted with correct alignment.

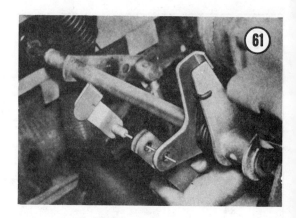

3. Adjust the accelerator cable length by turning the fork head while holding the nut with a wrench.

Transmission Removal/Installation

Figure 62 is an exploded diagram of the transmission case and associated parts.

1. Disconnect negative cable from battery.

2. Remove accelerator cable and detach it from counter thrust mounting, as shown in **Figure 63**.

3. Dismantle oil filler pipe and seal the opening.

4. Raise the car on hoist or jack it up and install jackstands.

5. Remove drain plug and drain oil into suitable container. Do not reuse oil.

6. Remove fixing bolts and exhaust supports from transmission.

7. Loosen the holder bracket. Remove bolts and disconnect exhaust pipe from exhaust manifold.

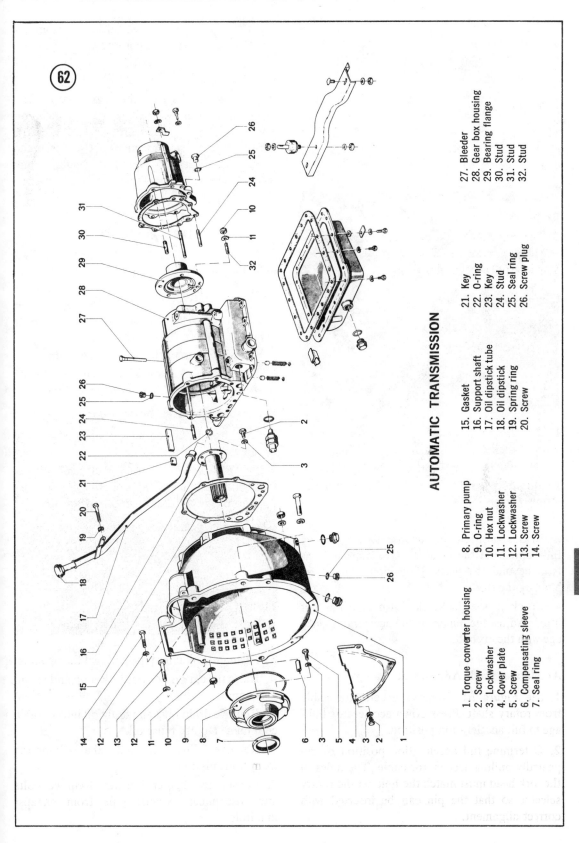

62

AUTOMATIC TRANSMISSION

1. Torque converter housing
2. Screw
3. Lockwasher
4. Cover plate
5. Screw
6. Compensating sleeve
7. Seal ring
8. Primary pump
9. O-ring
10. Hex nut
11. Lockwasher
12. Lockwasher
13. Screw
14. Screw
15. Gasket
16. Support shaft
17. Oil dipstick tube
18. Oil dipstick
19. Spring ring
20. Screw
21. Key
22. O-ring
23. Key
24. Stud
25. Seal ring
26. Screw plug
27. Bleeder
28. Gear box housing
29. Bearing flange
30. Stud
31. Stud
32. Stud

10

8. Disconnect drive shaft. Disconnect and remove drive shaft center bearing support.

9. Pull drive shaft downward and remove from centering journal.

10. Unscrew upper bolts fixing front of transmission to flywheel housing.

11. Disconnect speedometer drive shaft and selector rod, as shown in **Figure 64**. Remove cables from starter lock switch.

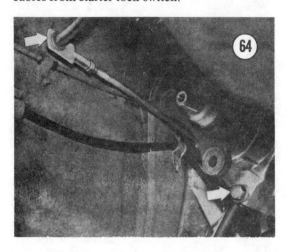

12. At the front of the transmission, loosen thrust bracket and dismantle cover plate by removing fixing bolts.

13. See **Figure 65**. Remove 4 bolts connecting torque converter to drive plate. Rotate the engine to gain access to each of the bolts.

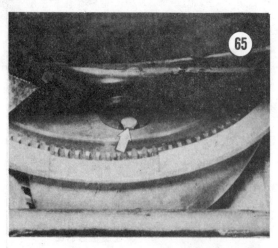

14. Support the transmission with a hydraulic jack and disconnect remaining fixing bolts from the transmission. Remove body crossmember.

15. Pull transmission backward away from engine. Extract the torque converter.

16. Lower the jack and remove from under the car.

17. To install, reverse the above steps. The torque converter is in the correct installation position when the guide journal is situated below the rim of the casing. If this is not so, insert the torque converter into the primary pump while turning gently.

DRIVE SHAFT

The drive shaft is balanced at the factory and must be renewed as an entire assembly. During disassembly, make certain to mark all parts of drive shaft and mating flanges relative to each other so that it can be assembled into a balanced unit.

Figure 66 is an exploded diagram of the drive shaft and associated parts.

Drive Shaft Removal/Installation

1. Disconnect the primary muffler from the exhaust pipe.

2. See **Figure 67**. Unscrew and remove nuts from bolts holding Giubo coupling from transmission flange. Withdraw nuts and washers.

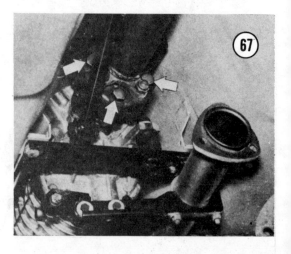

3. Remove nuts from differential/drive shaft mating flange, as shown in **Figure 68**. The nuts must be replaced with new ones during installation.

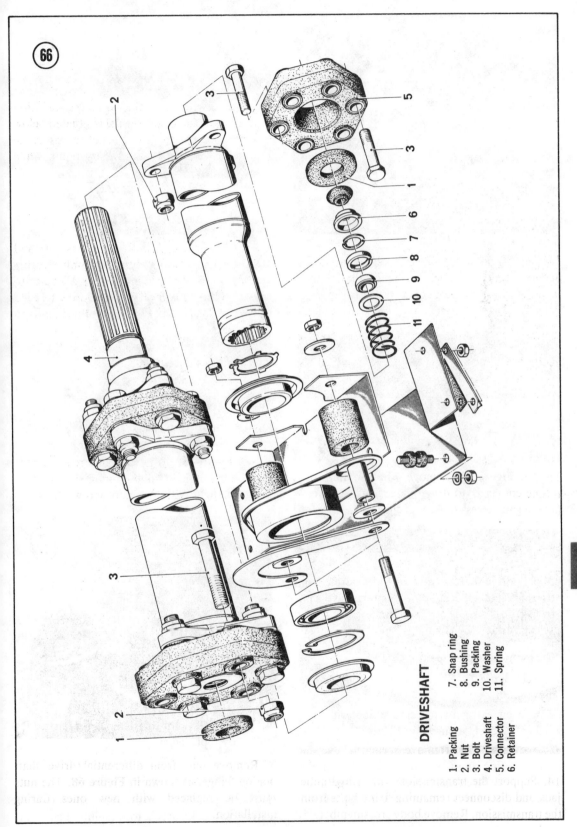

66

DRIVESHAFT

1. Packing
2. Nut
3. Bolt
4. Driveshaft
5. Connector
6. Retainer
7. Snap ring
8. Bushing
9. Packing
10. Washer
11. Spring

10

4. See **Figure 69**. Remove fixing bolts and disconnect center bearing. During installation, pretension center bearing forward (A) by approximately 0.08 in. (2mm).

5. Pull drive shaft downward and separate from transmission centering pin. Remove drive shaft from car.

Centering Ring Service

1. See **Figure 70**. Press out sealing cap and remove circlip.

2. Use an extractor to remove centering ring and ball socket, as shown in **Figure 71**.

3. See **Figure 72**. Remove spring (1), washer (2), centering ring (3), ball socket (4), retaining ring (5), and sealing cap. During installation, pack centering ring with approximately 6 grams of lubricant.

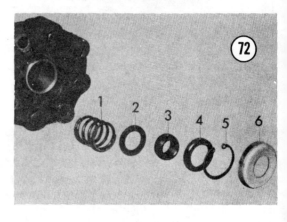

4. Inspect all parts for wear and damage. Repair is by replacement.

Center Bearing Removal/Installation

1. See **Figure 73**. Loosen and remove nut. Make certain to mark parts before pulling them apart.

2. With a puller, pull bearing off drive shaft.

3. Inspect bearing for wear and damage. Repair is by replacement.

4. Use a suitable drift to drive bearing onto drive shaft.

5. Some models are equipped with a sliding section, as shown in **Figure 74**. After removal of center bearing block, pull front drive shaft out of sliding section. Remove dust cap (7), circlip (4), ring (5), felt ring (1), toothed washer (2), and screw bushing (3). Pull off the bearing (6) with a puller. During installation, tighten screw bushing after installation in car.

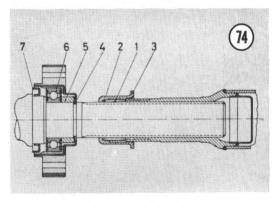

10

CHAPTER ELEVEN

BRAKES

This chapter provides maintenance information for the brake system, which consists of the fluid reservoir, master cylinder, power servo unit, front disc brakes, rear drum brakes, wheel cylinders, mechanical emergency brake, and necessary hoses and lines.

When working on the brake system, follow the general procedures below.

1. Exercise extreme cleanliness when handling parts.

2. Never touch rubber seals or internal hydraulic parts with greasy hands or rags.

3. Always use new, high quality brake fluid to clean hydraulic parts and to fill the reservoir. Never reuse fluid that has been bled from the hydraulic system.

4. Examine all seals carefully. If any damage is evident or suspected, replace with new parts.

5. Take care not to scratch the highly finished surfaces of cylinder bores and pistons.

Figure 1 is a hydraulic circuit diagram of the brake system. Tightening torques are given in **Table 1** at the end of the chapter.

BRAKE SYSTEM BLEEDING

Whenever any brake system work has been done or leaks discovered and repaired, the brake system must be bled to remove any air that may have entered. The front disc brake calipers have three bleed screws on each caliper and the rear drum brakes have one bleed screw on each wheel cylinder.

The bleeding sequence should be right rear, left rear, right front, and left front. Make certain to check the level of the fluid in the reservoir frequently during bleeding so that air will not be taken in through the master cylinder. Do not be satisfied that the bleeding sequence is completed until all signs of bubbles in the fluid have disappeared. If bubbles continue to appear after a reasonable time, there is a leak in the system that must be corrected before the car is driven.

1. Fill reservoir with brake fluid.

2. Remove all dirt and foreign material from around each bleed screw cover. After thorough cleaning, remove the covers.

3. See **Figure 2**. Install a tube to the bleed screw and immerse the lower end of the tube in a transparent container partly filled with brake fluid.

4. Loosen the bleed screw a few turns. Have an assistant press the brake pedal quickly and allow it to return slowly. Do this several times until no more air bubbles escape from the rubber tube.

5. When there are no more bubbles, hold down the brake pedal and tighten the bleed screw. Remove tube and replace protective cover.

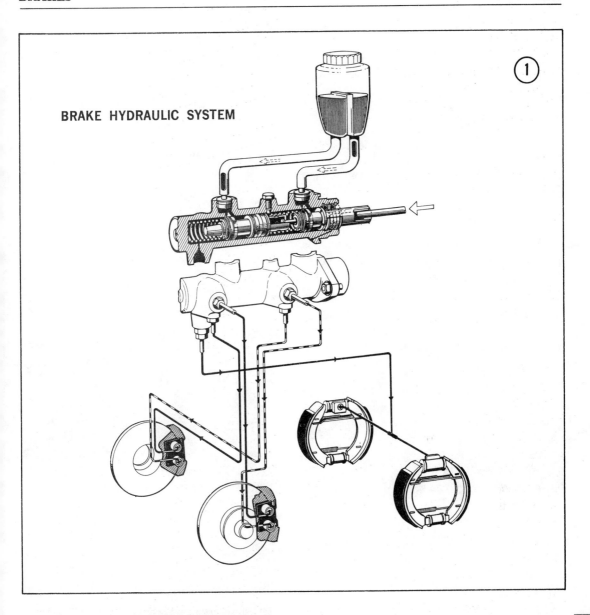

BRAKE HYDRAULIC SYSTEM

①

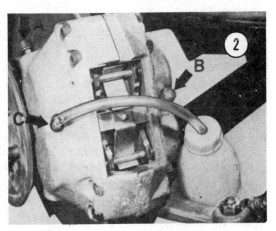

②

6. Repeat the bleeding operation for each wheel. When complete, fill the reservoir and road test the car.

MASTER CYLINDER

The master cylinder is of the tandem type and is linked to the front calipers and rear wheel cylinders to provide hydraulic pressure through the system. The pressure is activated by the driver through the brake pedal and power servo unit to the piston in the master cylinder. The pressure moves the piston and forces hydraulic fluid through the connecting lines and hoses.

Removal/Installation

1. Remove the reservoir cap and siphon off fluid to the level of the supply union to the master cylinder.

2. Loosen clamps and remove hydraulic lines at master cylinder. Mark for later replacement.

3. Remove nuts fixing master cylinder to power servo unit. Remove master cylinder from car. To install, reverse above steps, bleed lines, and replenish reservoir.

Overhauling

Overhaul repair kits are available and include parts most often found defective or that should be replaced after disassembly.

1. Remove master cylinder, as described above.

2. See **Figure 3**. Push in on piston (1) and remove stop screw (2). During installation, always replace copper sealing ring under stop screw.

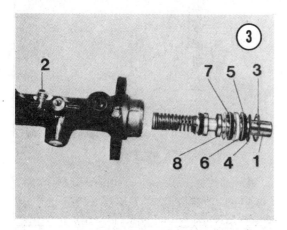

3. Remove circlip (3) and withdraw piston (1) from housing. Pull off washer (4), secondary sleeve (5), spacer ring (6), secondary sleeve (7), and washer (8). During installation, coat piston shank with silicone grease.

4. See **Figure 4.** Unscrew special screw (9) and remove spring cap (10), spring (11), spring cup (12), pressure cup (13), and O-ring (14). Always renew primary sleeve (8). During assembly, coat space between secondary sleeves (5, 7) and spacer ring with silicone grease, as shown in **Figure 5**.

5. See **Figure 6**. Use compressed air to push out piston (15). Pull off spring (16), spring cup (17),

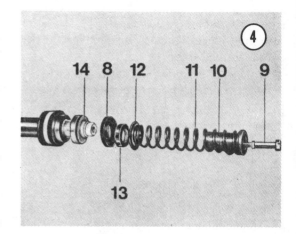

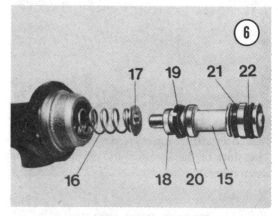

pressure cup (18), primary sleeve (19), and packing ring (20). Lift out secondary sleeve (21) and primary sleeve (22).

6. Clean all parts thoroughly. Inspect inner bore

of cylinder housing. If inner bore is scored or defective, replace with new unit. Make use of all parts included in repair kit.

7. Assemble master cylinder by reversing above steps. Be careful not to damage sleeves during insertion into the housing. After all parts have been inserted into housing, push in on piston and install stop screw.

POWER SERVO UNIT

The power servo unit is fitted to the brake pedal and the master cylinder. In case of failure, it is recommended that a new or reconditioned unit be installed. Whenever the master cylinder is removed, check the condition of the filter element as follows:

1. Remove master cylinder, as previously described.

2. See **Figure 7**. Remove dust cap (1), retainer ring (2), silencer (3), and filter (4).

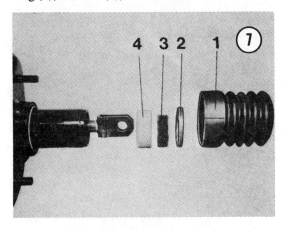

3. Clean the silencer and filter or replace with new parts.

4. To install, reverse the above steps. Locate the slots in the silencer and filter 180° from each other.

FRONT DISC BRAKES

The front disc brakes consist of the brake disc, 4-piston caliper, brake pads (linings), hydraulic lines, and other associated internal parts. The disc brakes do not require adjustment as they are self-adjusting. Wheel cylinders are not used as the caliper and pistons supply hydraulic pressure against the pads. Inspection of the pads should be done periodically to prevent damage to the brake disc through excessive wear. Always replace the pads for both front wheels at the same time.

Removal/Installation

1. Remove hub caps and loosen wheel nuts.

2. Jack up the car and support it with jack-stands. Remove wheel nuts and front wheels.

3. See **Figure 8**. Use a drift to drive out retaining pins.

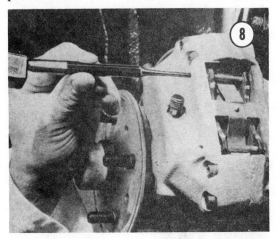

4. Pry out the cross spring (anti-rattle clip) from back side of caliper.

5. See **Figure 9**. Pull out the brake pads with extractor hook, as shown.

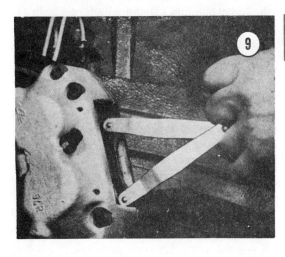

6. Measure the thickness of the pads. Minimum thickness is 0.276 in. (7.0mm). Replace the pads if worn excessively.

7. Inspect the brake discs (rotors) for burned spots and scoring. If defective, remove and overhaul or replace, as required. Instructions are given below.

8. Inspect caliper, pistons, and line connections for signs of leaks. If leaks are apparent, remove and overhaul or replace, as required.

9. Clean all parts thoroughly. Be careful not to contaminate brake pads with dirt, grease, or brake fluid.

10. To install pads, lower fluid level in reservoir and compress caliper pistons into caliper with piston reset pliers, as shown in **Figure 10**.

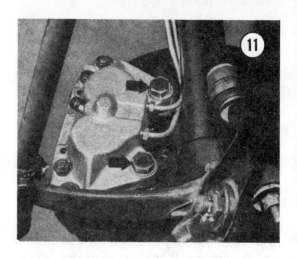

11. Fit pads to caliper. The brake disc must be able to rotate when pads are fitted. Replace cross spring, replenish reservoir, bleed brakes (if required), and replace road wheels. Road test the car at slow speeds. Avoid sudden stops for at least the first 300 miles to permit the pads to seat properly against the brake discs.

Caliper Removal/Installation

1. Remove the front wheels, as previously described.

2. Remove brake pads, as previously described.

3. Drain fluid from reservoir.

4. Unscrew and remove retaining bolts on back side of caliper, as shown in **Figure 11**.

5. Disconnect brake lines at caliper connection. Plug brake line ends to prevent loss of brake fluid and air entering the lines.

6. To install, reverse the above steps. Bleed brake lines on all wheels.

Overhaul

Overhaul repair kits are available for the caliper. All necessary parts are included in the repair kit as long as the caliper and pistons are not defective.

1. Remove brake pads and caliper.

2. See **Figure 12**. Lift off rubber caps from around pistons. Take care not to damage pistons.

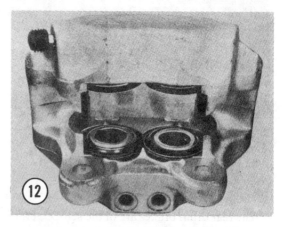

3. Press one piston into caliper stop with piston reset pliers. Use compressed air to force out piston opposite the one being held. Take care not to damage pistons as they are forced out. Repeat this step for all pistons.

4. See **Figure 13**. Remove sealing ring carefully. Clean cylinder bores and pistons thoroughly.

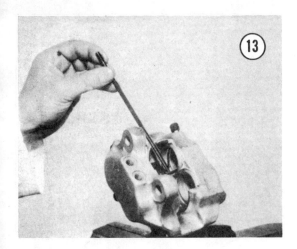

Check cylinder bore and pistons for wear, scoring, or damage. If defective, repair is by installation of new parts.

5. Further disassembly of the caliper is not recommended.

6. Assemble and install using reverse of steps above.

Brake Disc Removal/Installation

1. Remove the brake disc and wheel hub as described in Chapter Twelve.

2. Use a dial gauge to check runout of brake disc before it is removed. Maximum runout permissible is 0.002 in. (0.05mm).

3. Check the condition of the brake disc for scoring, burns, and damage. If defective, have the brake disc resurfaced. Minimum thickness of the brake disc is 0.354 in. (9.0mm). If resurfacing brings the brake disc to less than permissible thickness, replace with new one.

4. To install, reverse removal procedures.

REAR DRUM BRAKES

The rear drum brakes are of the self-centering type. Rear wheel cylinders supply hydraulic pressure to press the brake linings against the brake drums. Inspection of the brake linings should be done periodically to prevent damage to the brake drums through excessive wear. Always replace the linings for both wheels at the same time, regardless of condition. **Figure 14** (next page) shows the rear brake system.

Rear Brake Adjustment

Two adjusting nuts are provided on each wheel, as shown in **Figure 15**.

1. Jack up car and support it on jackstands. Release handbrake.

2. Rotate the road wheel in the forward direction. Use a spanner wrench on each adjusting nut at the same time. Simultaneously, turn the back nut counterclockwise and the front nut clockwise until the brake linings lock against the drum.

3. Loosen the adjusting nuts in the opposite directions until the wheel rotates freely without any drag.

Brake Lining Removal/Installation

1. Remove rear wheel hub caps and loosen wheel nuts. Release the handbrake.

2. Jack up car and support it on jackstands. Remove wheel nuts and wheels.

3. Pull the brake drum off of the wheel studs.

4. Remove cotter pin from axle shaft. Loosen and remove axle nut.

5. Use a puller, as shown in **Figure 16**, to pull off wheel drive flange.

6. On the back side of the brake assembly, loosen the adjusting nuts to loosen the brake shoes.

7. See **Figure 17**. Detach brake shoe spring at bottom of shoes.

8. Compress the brake shoes at the bottom and remove the top from the wheel cylinder.

11

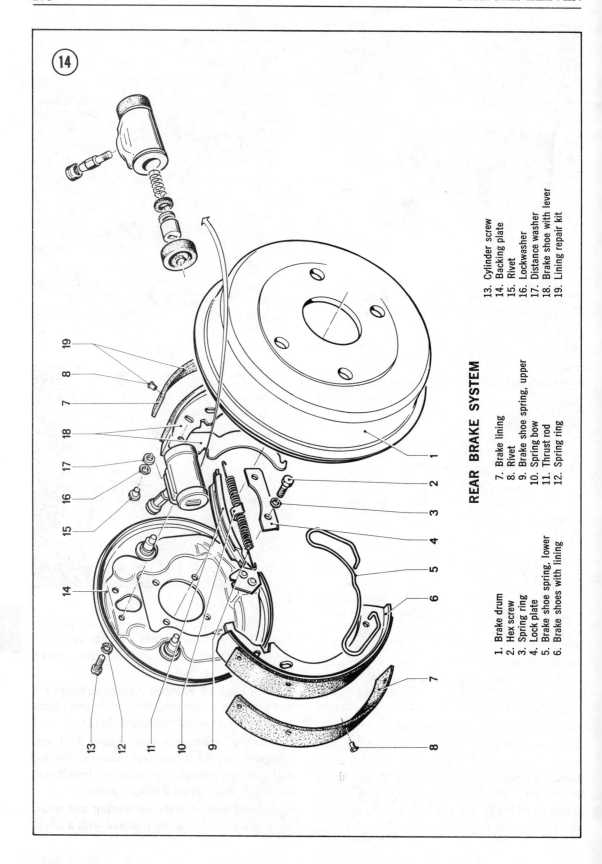

REAR BRAKE SYSTEM

1. Brake drum
2. Hex screw
3. Spring ring
4. Lock plate
5. Brake shoe spring, lower
6. Brake shoes with lining

7. Brake lining
8. Rivet
9. Brake shoe spring, upper
10. Spring bow
11. Thrust rod
12. Spring ring

13. Cylinder screw
14. Backing plate
15. Rivet
16. Lockwasher
17. Distance washer
18. Brake shoe with lever
19. Lining repair kit

9. Detach pushrod and handbrake cable.

10. Clean all parts thoroughly. Do not contaminate brake linings with grease, dirt, solvent, or brake fluid.

11. Inspect brake shoes for wear, damage, and signs of overheating. If the linings appear satisfactory, measure the lining thickness. Minimum allowable is 0.12 in. (3.0mm). Check that the lining has not worn so thin that the rivets are exposed to the brake drum. If the linings are not in excellent condition, reline the shoes or install new shoes with linings. Arc the linings to match the curvature of the brake drums.

12. Inspect the inside of the brake drums for wear, scoring, and overheating. If defective, have the drums turned and trued. Renew shoes to match drum oversize. Maximum inner diameter of brake drum is 7.87 to 7.91 in. (200 to 201mm) for the 1600 and 9.06 to 9.10 in.

(230 to 231mm) for the 2002 series. If the maximum inner diameter is exceeded, the drum must be replaced with a new one.

13. Check the condition of the wheel cylinder for signs of leaks. If any traces of brake fluid is found, remove and overhaul wheel cylinder, as discussed below.

14. To install brakes, reverse removal procedures. When installed, adjust brakes, as previously described, and adjust handbrake. Road test the car and adjust brakes as required.

Wheel Cylinder Overhaul

Repair kits are available for overhaul. Always use all parts included in repair kit.

1. Remove wheel, drum, and brake shoes, as described above.

2. See **Figure 18**. Unscrew and disconnect brake line from wheel cylinder. Plug end of brake line to prevent loss of brake fluid.

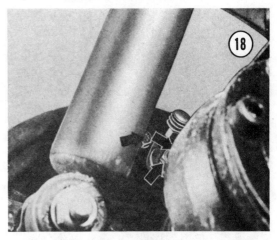

3. Unscrew bleed screw from wheel cylinder. Remove bolts fixing wheel cylinder to brake carrier. Remove wheel cylinder from brake carrier.

4. See **Figure 19**. Remove cylinder end caps (5) and withdraw pistons (4), sleeves (3), and piston spring (2) from wheel cylinder body (1).

5. Clean all parts with clean brake fluid and wipe dry. Inspect for damaged sleeves, pistons, and distorted springs. If satisfactory, install new sleeves. If not, replace damaged parts.

6. Inspect bore of body for scoring and wear. Very minor marks can be removed with a wheel

11

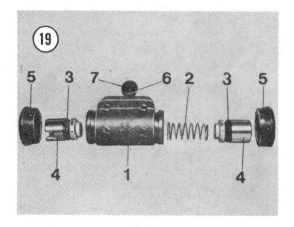

cylinder hone. Do not over-hone as leaks will result. If severely scored, use a new wheel cylinder body.

7. Assemble and install wheel cylinder using reverse procedure of removal. Install shoes, drum, and wheel. Road test the car and check carefully for brake fluid leaks.

Wheel Bearing Removal/Installation

1. Jack up the car and support with jackstands. Remove brake drum.

2. Remove bolts fixing axle to wheel flange. Tie axle up out of the way, as shown in **Figure 20**.

3. Partially thread on the nut to the wheel shaft and drive out the wheel shaft, as shown in **Figure 21**.

4. See **Figure 22**. Drive out ball bearing (2) and shaft sealing ring (1). Take out spacer sleeve (4) and shim (3). Drive out back bearing.

5. Clean all parts in suitable solvent. Inspect for wear and damage. Pay special attention to condition of ball bearing. If defective in any way, replace with new one.

6. Installation is the reverse of removal. If new parts are fitted or there is excessive play in the wheel, the shim must be replaced with one of the proper size. **Figure 23** shows measurements to be taken to determine shim size.

7. Pack the sealing lip and hub with grease.

HANDBRAKE

Adjustment

Handbrake adjustment should be done whenever the rear brakes are relined or when the handbrake lever can be pulled on to more than 4 teeth on the ratchet.

1. Adjust rear brakes, as previously described.

2. Push up rubber boot (1) on handbrake lever,

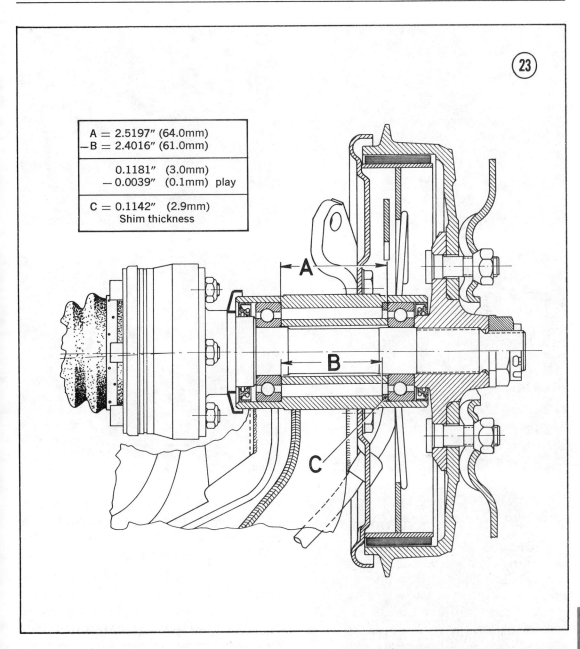

A = 2.5197" (64.0mm)
—B = 2.4016" (61.0mm)

0.1181" (3.0mm)
— 0.0039" (0.1mm) play

C = 0.1142" (2.9mm)
Shim thickness

as shown in **Figure 24**. Loosen locknut (2) and pull on handbrake until the fourth tooth is engaged. Tighten adjustment (3) while rotating rear wheel.

3. When the wheel locks, retighten the locknut.

4. Rotate the rear wheel with the handbrake lever released. The wheel should rotate freely. If not, readjust.

5. If both wheels do not lock at the same time, adjust the brake cable linkages to the wheel until they do.

BRAKE PEDAL

Adjustment/Servicing

1. See **Figure 25**. Remove retainer pin (2) and push out pin (3), after removing spring attached to pin.

2. Loosen locknut (5) and thread fork on shaft to adjust pedal. The brake pedal should be at the same height as the clutch pedal.

3. Inspect condition of pin and spring. Renew if damaged or distorted.

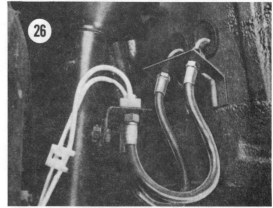

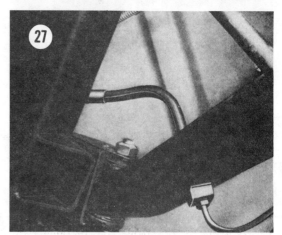

BRAKE LINES AND HOSES

Figure 26 shows the front brake hoses; **Figure 27** the rear. Whenever a brake line or hose is disconnected, take care not to twist or damage them as leaks may occur. A periodic inspection should be made of all lines, hoses, and unions.

1. Make certain metal lines are in perfect shape. Check for dents, cracks, and sharp corners.

2. Inspect rubber and canvas covered hoses to ensure they do not contact grease or anything that could wear on them. Work the brake pedal briskly and watch for balooning in the hoses, which could indicate weak spots.

3. Check support brackets to see that they are mounted securely. Constant car vibration can loosen them.

4. Check unions for leakage. Tighten or replace as required.

5. It is recommended that all hoses be replaced every 60,000 miles to help prevent sudden, catastrophic, failure.

Table 1   TORQUE TIGHTENING VALUES

	ft.-lb.
Fixed Caliper to Kingpin	58-69
Disc to Wheel Hub	43-48
Brake Hose	9.4-11.5
Brake Line Collar Nut	14.4-16.8
Brake Lever Thrust Rod Lock Nut	10.0-12.1
Master Cylinder/Power Servo Nut	9.4
Rear Wheel Drive Flange (shaft) Nut	217

CHAPTER TWELVE

FRONT SUSPENSION, WHEELS, AND STEERING

This chapter provides maintenance information on the front suspension, front wheels, and steering assemblies. Other than removal and replacement of assemblies and parts, the average owner/mechanic should refer major overhaul and adjustment of suspension or steering to a BMW dealer or specialist in this field. **Figure 1** shows the layout of components.

Before starting work on the front suspension, wheels, or steering, make certain the handbrake is firmly applied. Remove hub caps and loosen wheel nuts. Jack up the front of the car and support it with jackstands under frame. Remove wheel nuts and wheels. **Table 1** (end of the chapter) gives service data and specifications.

FRONT SUSPENSION

The front suspension is of the independent wishbone type with coil springs, telescopic hydraulic shock absorbers, and stabilizer bar. See **Figure 2**.

Front Axle Removal/Installation

1. See **Figure 3**. Remove bolts fixing calipers to guard plates. Detach caliper and tie up out of the way. Do not disconnect brake fluid lines.

2. See **Figure 4**. Remove bolt fixing angle to telescopic shock absorber.

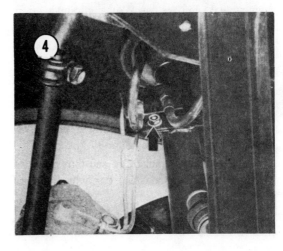

12

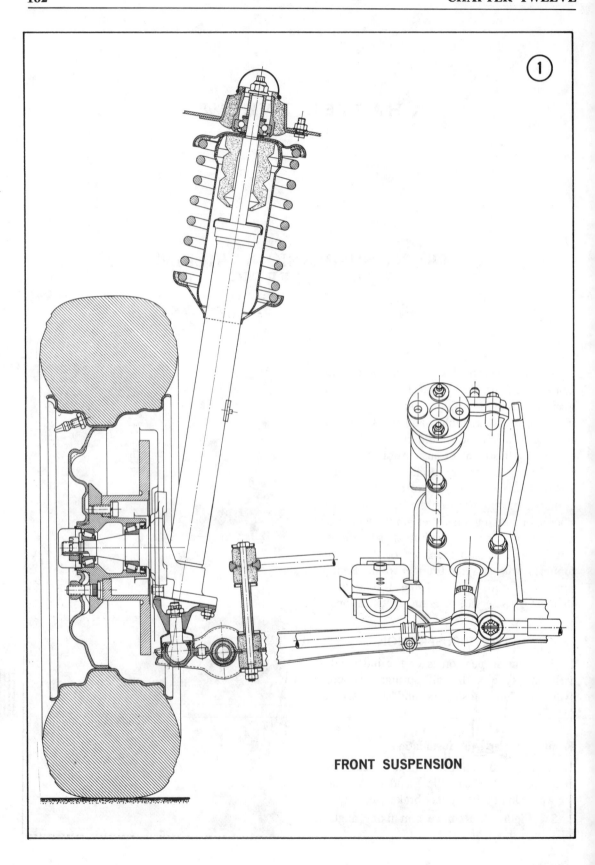

FRONT SUSPENSION

FRONT AXLE CARRIER

1. Hex screw
2. Castle nut
3. Cotter pin
4. Washer
5. Rubber mounting for stabilizing rod
6. Washer
7. Hex screw
8. Lockwasher
9. Spacer piece
10. Washer
11. Pipe
12. Stabilizing rod for front axle
13. Washer
14. Wishbone with rubber mounting
15. Rubber mounting for stabilizer rod, outer
16. Hex nut
17. Repair kit for track rod end

12

3. See **Figure 5**. Loosen bolts (1, 2) and remove bolt (2). Push universal joint upwards to its stop. During installation, the steering wheel and wheels must be in the straight forward position. The markings on the housing and pitman shaft must align with each other.

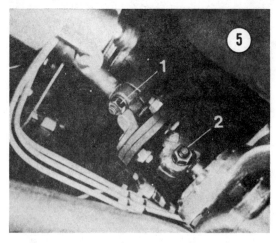

4. Loosen nuts and remove bolts fixing engine mounts to support plates.

5. See **Figure 6**. From inside engine compartment, loosen and remove nuts holding shock absorbers to wheel well.

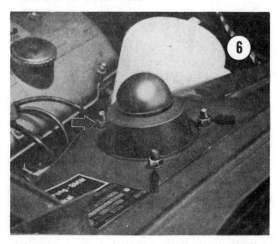

6. Support the engine with a hoist and lifting chains.

7. Place a hydraulic jack under the axle carrier. Use a lifting beam, such as shown in **Figure 7**, between the jack and axle carrier.

8. See **Figure 8**. Remove nuts and bolts and detach axle carrier from frame support.

9. Remove stabilizer bar, as described later under *Traction Strut Removal/Installation*.

10. See **Figure 9**. Remove cotter pin and remove nut and bolt fixing front traction struts. During installation the nut should be tightened finally with car in normal load position. Both washers must have the dome and faces against the axle carrier.

11. Remove bolts fixing wishbone to the front axle carrier. During installation, the nut should be tightened finally with car in normal load position. Install the spacer ring facing the axle carrier.

12. Press off the left-hand tie rod from the center tie rod with an extractor (6056). Press off center tie rod from drop arm with extractor (7009).

13. Remove bolts fixing steering gear from axle carrier. Tie the steering gear up to the brake servo unit.

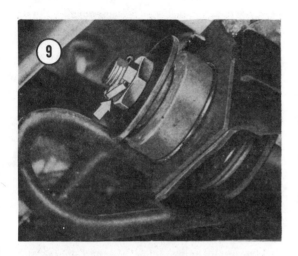

14. Remove cotter pin and nut and detach steering guide arm, as shown in **Figure 10**.

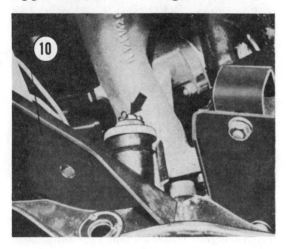

15. Lower jack under axle carrier and remove from under car.

Transverse Swing Arm Removal/Installation

1. Disconnect transverse swing arm from axle carrier by removing fixing bolts. Disconnect stabilizer from transverse swing arm.

2. Remove cotter pin and nut from steering knuckle arm. Use extractor (6056) to press off tie rod from steering knuckle.

3. Remove nut fixing traction strut to transverse swing arm. During installation, tighten nut finally with car under normal load. Both washers must mate with the curvatures on the transverse swing arm.

4. See **Figure 11**. Remove wire seal. Unscrew nuts and remove steering knuckle arm with transverse swing arm.

5. On the under side of the steering knuckle arm, remove cotter pin and nut.

6. Press off steering-knuckle arm from guide joint with an extractor.

Traction Strut Removal/Installation

1. Disassemble transverse swing arm from front axle carrier.

2. Disassemble the stabilizer from the transverse swing arm.

3. Detach traction strut at transverse swing arm.

4. Remove cotter pin and nut and detach traction strut at front axle beam.

5. During installation, tighten all nuts finally with car under normal load.

Front Suspension Servicing

1. Disassemble the front suspension as given above.

2. Inspect all parts carefully for wear, damage, cracks, and distortion. Pay special attention to condition of bushings and rubber bearings. Special equipment is required to press out and install bushings and bearings. Refer such service to your dealer or automotive machine shop.

3. The guide joint can be repaired by replacement of new joint onto bracket. Use a drill to remove rivet heads and knock out rivets with a punch. Install new guide joint to bracket and secure with nuts and bolts.

12

4. The rubber bearings on the stabilizer and transverse swing arm can be replaced by disassembling the joints and pulling the bearings from their mountings. Make certain to tighten joints tightly enough to distort rubber bearing so that the stabilizer and transverse swing arm cannot slip from position. Make certain to install locknuts.

WHEEL BEARINGS

Removal/Installation

1. See Figure 3. Remove bolts fixing calipers to guard plate.

2. Detach angle plate from shock absorber.

3. Detach the caliper and tie up out of the way. Do not disconnect brake lines.

4. Remove cotter pin from axle shaft and remove axle shaft nut.

5. Pull off brake disc and wheel hub.

6. On the back side of the wheel hub, remove socket head screws fixing wheel hub to brake disc. This step is only necessary if the wheel hub or brake disc require repair or replacement.

7. See **Figure 12**. Lift out the axle sealing ring and remove taper roller bearing. Pull out bearing outer races with extractor or drive out bearing outer races through the recesses in the wheel hub with a suitable drift.

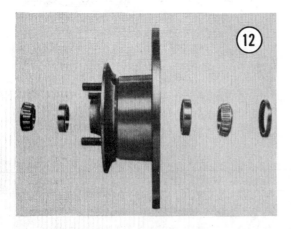

8. Inspect all parts for wear and damage. If the bearings are pitted or do not rotate freely, replace with new ones. If one bearing needs to be replaced, replace both of them. Always replace seals.

9. Press bearing outer races into place with a suitable drift, after lubricating with wheel bearing grease.

10. Pack the axle shaft seal with grease. Fill the hub cap with grease. Adjust the wheel bearing, as discussed below, and install the hub cap to the wheel hub.

Adjustment

1. Remove and install wheel bearings, as discussed above.

2. Thread nut onto axle shaft.

3. Continuously turn wheel hub and tighten nut to 7.2 ft.-lb. to align the bearing inner races and to equalize grease pressure.

4. Loosen the nut 1/3 turn. Rotate wheel hub and check for freedom of movement. It must not bind or drag. Make certain to rotate in both directions. Install cotter pin and bend ends around axle shaft.

5. Use a dial gauge to check the end play in the wheel hub and the bearings. Acceptable end play is 0.0008 to 0.0024 in. (0.02 to 0.06mm).

SHOCK ABSORBER/COIL SPRING

Removal/Installation

1. Remove caliper, angle plate, wheel hub, and brake disc, as described above.

2. See **Figure 13**. Loosen and remove bolts fixing guard plate. Remove guard plate.

3. See **Figure 14**. Remove cotter pin and nut fixing tie rod. Press off tie rod with extractor (6056), as shown.

4. Disconnect transverse swing arm from front axle carrier.

5. See Figure 11. Remove wire seal and disconnect tie rod lever from shock absorber.

6. Remove nuts from bolts fixing upper end of shock absorber to wheel well.

7. Withdraw shock absorber assembly (including coil spring) from car.

8. Compress the coil spring with a spring clamp to remove spring tension.

9. See **Figure 15**. Remove cap from upper end of shock absorber assembly. Unscrew nut from shock absorber shaft and remove washers and bushing.

10. Inspect all parts for wear and damage. Check the coil spring carefully and replace with

new one, if defective. If the shock absorber is defective, replace it with a rebuilt unit or have your dealer install a repair kit to overhaul.

11. Always replace shock absorbers and coil springs as a set to maintain correct wheel and suspension stability.

12. Installation is the reverse procedure of removal.

WHEEL ALIGNMENT

Due to the specialized equipment required, wheel alignment should be referred to a BMW dealer. Before having the wheels aligned, the following services or checks should be made.

1. Check that tire pressure is correct.

2. Check end play of front wheel bearings, as discussed above.

3. Check and adjust steering, as required.

4. Check condition of bushings and rubber bearings in suspension system. Service as required.

5. Check shock absorber efficiency and service, as required.

Specifications for front wheel alignment are given at the end of this chapter.

STEERING

The steering gear is of the worm and roller type, with a ratio of 17.6 to 1. The steering box is mounted on the inside wall of the engine compartment. **Figure 16** is an exploded diagram of the steering box. Major overhaul of the steering system should be referred to your BMW dealer or specialist in this field. The following provides information for removal, disassembly, adjustment, and installation of the steering gear.

Steering Box Removal/Installation

1. See **Figure 17**. Mark the position of the upper joint flange relative to the steering shaft.

2. See **Figure 18**. Loosen upper bolt (1). Remove nut and bolt (2). During installation the steering column bearing must be preloaded by 0.08 to 0.1 in. (2.0 to 2.5mm). Press firmly down on the steering wheel to achieve the preload. Be certain that bolt (2) seats in the steering shaft groove.

12

⑯

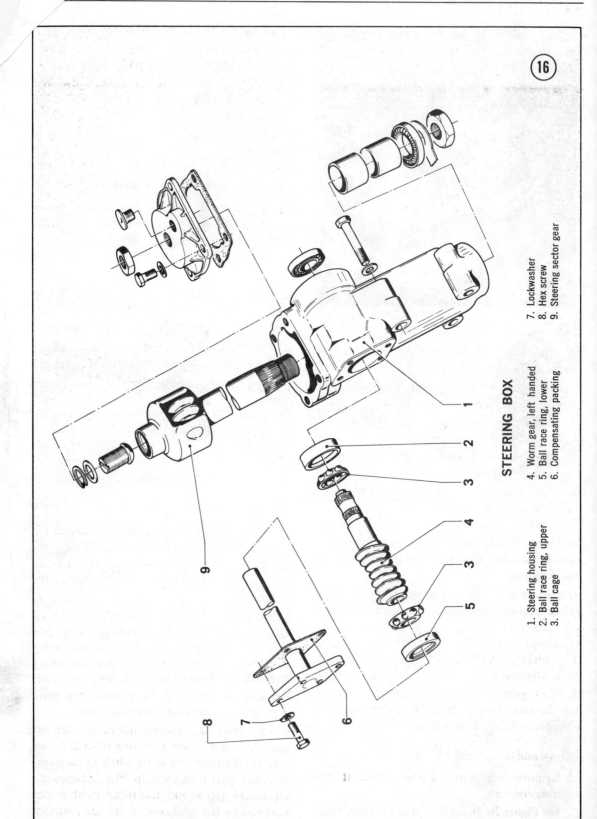

STEERING BOX

1. Steering housing
2. Ball race ring, upper
3. Ball cage
4. Worm gear, left handed
5. Ball race ring, lower
6. Compensating packing
7. Lockwasher
8. Hex screw
9. Steering sector gear